## walking with purpose

Dear Friend,

I wrote *Ordering Your Priorities* in the middle of a worldwide pandemic. I, like most people, felt off-kilter, and very aware of all that I could not control. I found myself strategizing how I could buy toilet paper, hand sanitizer, and yeast (there was a lot of baking going on in those months). Events we had been looking forward to were canceled, children came home (the adult ones, too), and we experienced more togetherness than we had in years. Some of this was refreshing and restorative. But it also brought with it a tremendous amount of stress.

During this time, I noticed that global rates of drinking were skyrocketing. Clearly, the stress had gotten to us all. The uncertainty was just too unsettling. The rug had been pulled out from under everyone and we weren't quite sure what we were supposed to do next. We didn't know how to unwind, how to mark the days, how to deal with all the things we didn't like about our current circumstances.

What I personally found to be a game changer in this season was to go back to the basics—to return to what I had always said was most important. Almost a decade ago, I wrote the book *Walking with Purpose: Seven Priorities That Make Life Work*. It was the truths contained in that book that gave me an anchor in the midst of this period of uncertainty. I went back to those principles and found that they tethered me, gave structure to my day, and settled my heart. They still rang true.

Reading just the right book at just the right time can be truly life-changing. But transformation goes to a whole new level when we participate in the learning process. When we do the work of opening our Bibles, digging for the truth ourselves, inviting the Holy Spirit to instruct us, we are changed in a lasting way. Because of this, I decided to take the principles of my book and turn it into a Bible study.

But as always happens when I write, God had some new lessons to teach me. I found that with each priority, He had a fresh message and new application for my current circumstances. That means this Bible study and *Walking with Purpose: Seven Priorities That Make Life Work* are complementary, but not repetitive.

As I reflect on the rising rates of anxiety, depression, alcohol consumption, Netflix bingeing, and online escapism, I am arrested by the following question: Instead of needing to escape our lives, how about if we build a life we don't want to escape?

That is what I've set out to help you do in *Ordering Your Priorities*. I will provide you food for thought, questions for reflection, and truths to ponder. But you will have to do the work. That is my prayer for you and me, that we would apply the principles contained in this study and create a life we don't need to escape. In John 10:10, Jesus said, "I came that you might have life, and have it abundantly." That is what we are pursuing here.

With you on the journey,

Lisa

**Lisa Brenninkmeyer**
**Founder and Chief Purpose Officer, Walking with Purpose**

# Ordering Your Priorities

*Building a Life Well Lived*

# ORDERING YOUR PRIORITIES

## Building a LIFE Well Lived

## Lisa Brenninkmeyer

**walking with purpose**

~ SO MUCH MORE THAN A BIBLE STUDY ~

www.walkingwithpurpose.com

Authored by Lisa Brenninkmeyer

**IMPRIMATUR**        ✝ Frank J. Caggiano, Bishop of Bridgeport
                        August 15, 2021

The recommended Bible translations for use in Walking with Purpose studies are: The New American Bible, which is the translation used in the United States for the readings at Mass; The Revised Standard Version, Catholic Edition; and The Jerusalem Bible.

22 23 24 25 / 12 11 10 9 8 7 6 5 4 3 2

ISBN: 978-1-943173-35-8

Ordering Your Priorities: Building a Life Well Lived

Printed in the United States of America

# TABLE OF CONTENTS

## INTRODUCTION

## LESSONS

## APPENDICES

## ANSWER KEY

## PRAYER PAGES

# Welcome to Walking with Purpose

You have many choices when it comes to how you spend your time—thank you for choosing Walking with Purpose. Studying God's Word with an open and receptive heart will bring spiritual growth and enrichment to all aspects of your life. Every moment you invest will be well worth it.

Each of us comes to this material with a unique vantage point. You are welcome as you are. No previous experience is necessary. Some of you will encounter questions that introduce you to concepts that are new. For others, much of the content will be a review. God meets each one of us where we are. He is always faithful, taking us to a deeper, better spiritual place, no matter where we begin.

## The Structure of *Ordering Your Priorities*

*Ordering Your Priorities* is an eight-session Bible study that integrates Scripture with the teachings of the Roman Catholic Church to answer the core question, "What is God's vision for our life, and how can I experience it?" We will discover that God is our true north, and through Him, the path to rightly ordered priorities and a life well lived. This Bible study is designed for both interactive personal study and group discussion.

For those who are participating in Walking with Purpose in a group context, six weeks of this study will be spent in small groups discussing one of the lessons from the *Ordering Your Priorities* Bible study guide. During two additional weeks participants will gather for a Connect Coffee, which consists of social time, a video presentation of the related Bible study talk, and small group discussion. Anyone doing this study on her own will find it simplest to watch the videos online, using the URLs provided with the talk outlines.

## Study Guide Format and Reference Materials

The *Ordering Your Priorities* Bible study guide is divided into three sections:

The first section comprises eight lessons. Most lessons are divided into five "days" to help you form a habit of reading and reflecting on God's Word. If you are a woman who has only bits and pieces of time throughout your day to accomplish tasks, you will find this breakdown of the lessons especially helpful. Each lesson includes an introduction; a conclusion; a resolution section, in which you set a goal for yourself based on a theme of the lesson; and portions of the *Catechism of the Catholic Church (CCC)* that are referenced in the lesson.

For the two Connect Coffee talks in the series, accompanying outlines are offered as guides for taking notes. Questions are included to guide your group's discussion following the video.

The second section, the appendices, contains supplemental materials referred to during the study, as well as an article about Saint Thérèse of Lisieux, the patron saint of Walking with Purpose.

The third section contains the answer key. You will benefit so much more from the Bible study if you work through the questions on your own, searching your heart. This is your very personal journey of faith. The answer key is meant to supplement discussion or provide some guidance when needed.

At the end of the book are pages intended for weekly prayer intentions.

## Bible Recommendations

What were your thoughts the first time you picked up a Bible? Perhaps you got one as a gift for Confirmation or graduation. Maybe it was a copy you found lying around at home. It could be that the first time you held a Bible was in a classroom setting. Which of these two statements better reflects how you felt in that moment: "I just can't wait to dive into these pages because I know it'll be life-changing" or "This looks boring and inaccessible. I'm sticking it on my shelf"? For most of us, it was the latter.

One of our goals at Walking with Purpose is to teach women how to use the Bible as a practical, accessible tool. There are some obstacles to that happening. One problem is how we approach the Bible. If we open it up to Genesis and start reading through from start to finish, we will likely have trouble understanding what is going on (and we'll probably quit once we get into Leviticus). One of the reasons this method can be confusing is because Scripture is not a book; it's a library. This library is filled with many genres: poetry, letters, historical narrative, and apocalyptic writings. When we don't know what genre we are reading, we can quickly become frustrated. For example, reading Genesis as a science book instead of as inspired poetry will cause us to see faith and science at odds. Far too many people write off Christianity because they feel it can't possibly be true after seeing discrepancies between things proven by science and the way those same things are described in the Bible. This is a consequence of not recognizing the Bible as a *library* of Truth, utilizing many genres of literature to lead us to the heart of God, understand His story, and see our place in the epic tale of redemption. Catholics don't read everything in the Bible literally. We read some things literally, but not everything.

Another obstacle to using the Bible as a practical, accessible tool for spiritual growth is not knowing where to begin. This is exactly why Walking with Purpose has created Bible studies and programs like BLAZE. Being guided through Scripture, being led to the passages that are most applicable to life in the twenty-first century, helps the Bible to come alive.

You may also want to consider Bible tabs as a resource. It takes about thirty minutes to put tabs into a Bible, but it makes it so much easier to find your way around Scripture. You can find Bible tabs at Catholic bookstores or online. Be sure to get the Catholic version, as Protestant versions of the Bible are missing seven books. (At the time of the Reformation, the books of Sirach, Tobit, Wisdom, Judith, 1 and 2 Maccabees, and Baruch, as well as portions of Daniel and Esther, were removed in order to embrace a canon of Scripture that reflected Protestant theological beliefs. Books were never *added* to the Catholic Bible—they have always been there.)

We recommend using either the NABRE (New American Bible Revised Edition) or the RSVCE (Revised Standard Version, Catholic Edition) translations.

## Walking with Purpose™ Website

Please visit our website at www.walkingwithpurpose.com to find additional free content, supplemental materials that complement our Bible studies, as well as a link to our online store for additional Bible studies, DVDs, books, and more!

*WWP Scripture Printables* of our exclusively designed verse cards that compliment all Bible studies. They are available in various sizes and formats, perfect for lock screens or emailing to a friend.

*WWP Playlists* of Founder Lisa Brenninkmeyer's favorite music accompany each Bible study.

***WWP Videos*** of all Connect Coffee talks.

***WWP Blog*** for a weekly dose of inspiration and encouragement from our bloggers. Subscribe for updates.

***WWP Leadership Development Program***

Do you long to see more women touched by the love of Christ, but you aren't sure how you can help? We are here to help you learn the art of creating community. It's easier than you think! God doesn't call the equipped; He equips the called. If you love God and love women, then you have what it takes to make a difference in the lives of people around you. Through our training, you'll be empowered to step out of your comfort zone and experience the rush of serving God with passion and purpose. You are not alone, and you can become a great leader. We offer the encouragement and the tools you need to reach out to a world that desperately needs to experience the love of God.

**Join Us on Social Media**

facebook.com/walkingwithpurpose

twitter.com/walkingwpurpose

instagram.com/walkingwithpurpose_official

youtube.com/walkingwithpurpose_official

pinterest.com/walkingwpurpose

# Lessons

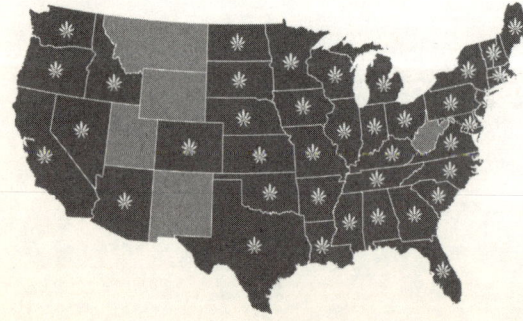

Walking with Purpose is a community of women growing in faith – together! This is where women are gathering. Join us!

www.walkingwithpurpose.com

# Lesson 1: Connect Coffee Talk 1

## BUILDING THE GOOD LIFE

Accompanying talk can be viewed via DVD or digital download purchase, or access online at walkingwithpurpose.com/videos.

*"The thief comes only to steal and kill and destroy; I came that they may have life, and have it abundantly." (John 10:10)*

I.  **Building Your Life on the Rock**

      Matthew 7:24–27

      Luke 14:28–30

      Genesis 11:1–4

      Jeremiah 6:16

      Psalm 61:1–3

II. **Principle 1: People Over Projects**

      2 Corinthians 4:18

## III. **Principle 2: The Hierarchy of Relationships**

    A.  God

        Psalm 139:1–16

    B.  Husband

    C.  Children

    D.  Extended Family

    E.  Friends

        The Four Circles of Friendship

**Circle of Concern** ⟶

**Circle of Influence** ⟶

**Circle of Intimacy** ⟶

**Center: God** ⟶

# Discussion Questions:

1.  Which priorities compete for first place in your life? In what ways do you experience the tyranny of the urgent—the temptation to put projects before people?

2.  Do you see evidence in our culture of the loss of a basic understanding of what it means to be human? In which ways specifically? What is one concrete action you could take to step away from isolating habits and toward healthy community?

3.  Remembering that it isn't a matter of good people and bad people, but the flow of influence, reflect on who is in your Four Circles of Friendship. Do you feel that the friends in your circle of influence are helping you to love better? Why or why not? Are there any changes you want to make regarding which friendships warrant a greater or lesser investment of your time?

Thus says the Lord; STAND BY THE ROADS, AND LOOK, AND ask FOR the ANCIENT Paths, where the GOOD WAY is; and WALK in it, and find REST for Your Souls.

Jeremiah 6:16

# Lesson 2:

# PRIORITY 1: YOUR RELATIONSHIP WITH GOD

## Introduction

*"God loved you before you were born, and God will love you after you die. In Scripture, God says, 'I have loved you with an everlasting love.' This is the fundamental truth of your identity. This is who you are, whether you feel it or not. You belong to God from eternity to eternity. Life is just a little opportunity for you during a few years to say, 'I love you too.'"* —Henri Nouwen

The greatest yearning of the human heart is to be loved in such a way that we have a sense of belonging, experience being known, and feel safe. Because God wired us for connection—He created us to be in relationship—our greatest fear is being rejected or abandoned. So many of the things we are afraid of, when boiled down to their essence, are connected to this fear of ultimately being alone in the face of uncertainty.

This means we don't want to merely survive or succeed. Our longings run far deeper than that. While one might spend the majority of one's time pursuing achievements and financial security, in the end, those things never satisfy. It is the quality of our relationships that determines the quality of our lives.

The difficulty comes in figuring out how to find that kind of love and how to receive it. So many of us don't know how to love or be loved by God because we have been hurt in the past by people who were supposed to love us well. Hard as we might try, we don't keep things nearly as compartmentalized as we'd like. Hurts from one relationship can flow over into another, without our ever intending it.

British psychiatrist John Bowlby spent his life researching the ways in which our early attachments significantly impact future relationships. He found that there are four things integral to healthy attachment:

---

1    Henri J. M. Nouwen, *Finding My Way Home: Pathways to Life and the Spirit* (Chestnut Ridge, NY: Crossroad, 2018), 129.

- We monitor and maintain emotional and physical closeness.
- We reach out for this person when we are unsure, upset, or feeling down.
- We miss him or her when we're apart.
- We count on this person when we step out into the unknown.[2]

When a child's need for attachment is not met, he or she will develop coping mechanisms to deal with the pain. Those coping mechanisms (becoming demanding and controlling or turning away and shutting down one's needs[3]) are carried into adulthood and impact adult relationships. They also impact one's relationship with God.

In this lesson, we are going to explore how to experience a relationship with God in our day-to-day lives. For some of you, it won't be difficult to believe in God's relentless, never-ending, very personal love. But many of you will battle a voice in your head that says, "That love might be available to some people, but it's not for me." You'll find it hard to apply the verses you read to yourself. The more we have been hurt, the harder it is to receive God's love. *Harder*, yes, but not impossible.

I must acknowledge, I don't know your story. I don't know the ways you have been let down and betrayed in the past. I don't know how many times you have hoped to be loved well and found yourself deeply disappointed. I don't know how high the walls are around your heart or how you may have vowed never to risk being hurt again. But one thing I do know: God knows your story. He has been there, in every moment of it. He has never left you. His eyes have always been on you, and at the very times when you have felt most alone, He has leaned in and held you.

His is the voice deep within that calls you His beloved. He has not demanded that you prove worthy of such love. That love is offered to you simply because you are His precious daughter. He sees your innermost self and does not recoil. He meets you with mercy at your point of greatest weakness and failure.

At this very moment, God is pursuing you. He longs to break through the barriers that are blocking you from experiencing His love, but He is a gentleman. He will not force His way in. He stands at the door of your heart, not with a list of rules and regulations, but with open arms. Do you notice that it is God taking the initiative? He approaches you with a heart full of kindness and mercy and invites you to draw near.

---

2   Dr. Sue Johnson with Kenneth Sanderfer, *Created for Connection: The "Hold Me Tight" Guide for Christian Couples* (New York: Little, Brown Spark, 2016), 25.

3   Johnson and Sanderfer, *Created for Connection*, 30.

## Day One
## RECEIVE GOD'S LOVE

*"Is God a masterful physician who diagnoses from afar? Or is he someone who has gone to the scene of disease or famine and attended close hand? Or is he someone who, when he attends, really knows what he is doing because he has first caught the disease and starved from the hunger?"*[4] —*Father Iain Matthew*

1. At the heart of a good relationship is trust. And in order to trust someone, we need to understand something of who that person is. What does 1 John 4:16 reveal about God?

   How did God show His love to us? See John 3:16 and Romans 5:8.

   What do we learn about God from John 1:18?

2. Jesus is often referred to as the Great Physician, and He is not one who diagnoses from afar. Stepping down from His throne in heaven, He "dwelt among us" (John 1:14). He moved into the neighborhood. He got as close as He possibly could.

   God knew that the disease of sin was killing His children. What did He do about it? See 2 Corinthians 5:21.

   Jesus, who lived a sinless life, allowed all our sins to be placed on Him on the cross. He fully felt the effects of the disease of sin and offered Himself as the cure.

   To read more background on this verse, see Appendix 2: The Divine Exchange.

3. To trust others, it helps to know where they stand in relation to us. Are they close enough to be relied upon? When they show up, are they consistent? Do they offer a safe haven or are we not sure of the kind of reception we'll receive? Read the following Bible verses, noting what they reveal about God's posture toward us.

---

4  Father Iain Matthew, *The Impact of God* (London, UK: Hodder and Stoughton, 1995), 115.

Psalm 68:5–6


Psalm 91:1–4


Jeremiah 31:3


Revelation 3:20



4. God's relationship to us is described many ways in Scripture, and they all speak of attachment. God is the Father; we are His children. God is the vine; we are the branches. God is the shepherd; we are the sheep. One of the most intimate descriptions is that of God as the bridegroom and us as the bride. This is the theme of the book Song of Solomon (or Song of Songs, in some translations). Although God is never mentioned in the book, it is all about His love for us. This book of the Bible has been the favorite of many saints, including Saint John of the Cross, Saint Thomas Aquinas, and Saint Bernard of Clairvaux. Read the following verses from Song of Solomon, and comment on the love relationship described.

Song of Solomon 1:15–16



Song of Solomon 2:4



Song of Solomon 8:6–7

*Quiet your heart and enjoy His presence…He is closer than you can imagine.*

*"Why did God create you? He created billions of other people; were they not enough for him? No, they were not. He had to have you. He will not rest until he has you home. Even if you are the one sheep that is lost, he will leave the ninety-nine (or ninety-nine billion) others to seek you wherever you are. He will come into your thickets and your wilderness and your suffering and even, on the Cross, your sin. "For our sake he made him to be sin who knew no sin, so that in him we might become the righteousness of God" (2 Cor 5:21). One of the splinters on the Cross that pierced his flesh was yours alone. And one of the gems in his crown will be yours alone."[5] —Peter Kreeft*

*If only you could truly grasp the depth of God's love for you. If you could, it would satisfy your every longing. It is He that you were born hungering for, hunting for, searching for. Your life is actually a love story, no matter how disappointed you may have been by people falling short. The One who pursues you is the Lover of your soul. He isn't asking you to prove that you are worth something. You don't have to do something spectacular or relevant or fantastic in order to earn His love. It's offered as a gift, and He proved that He meant it when He died for you on the cross. Lean into this fundamental truth about your value and your identity. Open your hands, open your heart, and invite Him in. In the words of Henri Nouwen, "Life is just a little opportunity for you during a few years to say, 'I love you too.'"[6]*

---

5    Peter Kreeft, *Three Philosophies of Life* (San Francisco, CA: Ignatius Press, 1989), 124.
6    Nouwen, *Finding My Way Home*, 129.

# Day Two
## RECOGNIZE HIS VOICE

*"You've owned your fear and all your self-loathing
You've owned the voices inside of your head
You've owned the shame and reproach of your failure
It's time to own your belovedness"*[7] *—Sarah Kroger*

1.  A.  It would be great if our thoughts were always in line with God's perspective, but unfortunately the voices inside our heads all too often contradict it. What does John 10:27 tell us about who is able to discern God's voice?

    B.  The starting point for recognizing God's voice is behaving as sheep with a shepherd. What additional insights do you gain into this dynamic from John 10:1–5?

    C.  We all like to think that we are far smarter than sheep. But isn't it interesting that sheep are smart enough to not follow a stranger who doesn't know their names, while we have trouble in that area? Those who climb into the sheep pen are thieves and robbers. The same can be said of the voices in our heads that feed our self-loathing and cause us to feel that we are never enough. Those voices rob us of joy and peace and lead us to discouragement and sometimes despair. God's voice is very different. Read Isaiah 43:1–2 as God speaking directly to you. Note what these words mean to you personally.

2.  A.  Reflect on the voices in your head. There are thoughts and voices competing with God's. Can you think of people in your life whose voices have exerted a strong influence? List them here. Note which voices have blessed and which have condemned. If you can think of a specific message given, a name spoken over you, record it next to the person who spoke it.

---

7   Sarah Kroger, "Belovedness," from the album *Light* (Nashville, TN: Integrity Music, 2020), https://genius.com/Sarah-kroger-belovedness-lyrics.

B. What do we learn from Isaiah 55:8–9 about the difference between God's thoughts and our own?

The higher thoughts—those that belong to God—are thoughts fueled by a perspective that we don't have on this side of eternity. Your memory is limited, but God can remember when He made you. He knows all the gifts and potential He placed inside you. When you ended up with traits that make you different, that's not some kind of mistake. That was God's plan all along. He likes you exactly as He made you.

3. We can easily fall into two different errors. One is thinking that God's voice is always corrective. The other is thinking that He is continuously saying, "Just be yourself! No need to change!" The truth is found in the middle. He sees your inherent dignity and worth, and nothing you do can make Him love you more or less. But God loves you too much to leave you as you are. So sometimes His voice tells you about things that need to change. The following two verses can help us discern if a voice that sounds corrective is His.

A. Why did God send Jesus into the world? See John 3:17.

God did not send us Jesus so that we would feel condemned. The enemy's voice is one of *condemnation*. By contrast, God's is one of *conviction*. He convicts us in order to save us.

B. What is Scripture useful for? See 2 Timothy 3:16.

Scripture is one of the primary ways God speaks to us. His voice bounces off the pages of the Bible and into our hearts. The Bible has been given to us for many reasons, and one of them is the way in which it can teach us. In 2 Timothy 3:16 it is described as a teaching tool, a way that we can be discipled. The words are not meant to condemn, but to convict us of our sin and teach us a better way to live. When we are convicted of sin, our behavior is addressed. By contrast, when we are condemned, we feel our dignity is brought into question. With God, your dignity is never on the line. But His conviction is a gift that helps you see where you have veered off the path leading to the good life.

4.  A.  There's a powerful story in 1 Kings 19 about the prophet Elijah. He had poured out his life for God and was being chased by a powerful enemy as a result. Exhausted and afraid, Elijah fled to a cave in the mountains. He was desperate for a word from God, and God met him there. He told Elijah to go to the mouth of the cave. A great and strong wind passed by, but God wasn't in the wind. Then there was an earthquake, but God wasn't in the earthquake. Next came a fire, but God wasn't in the fire either. But after all the noise, God spoke in "a still, small voice" (1 Kings 19:12). If we want to hear God's voice, Psalm 46:10 tells us what is necessary. Share this insight here.

God speaks in the still, small whisper. This means we must get quiet. It means to stop talking. To switch off our phones. To stop arguing, questioning, and complaining. To stop commenting and to listen instead. It's worth noting that listening is not the same as reading social media comments.

An insight from a friend changed the way author Laura Phelps structured her prayer time. "'Have you been silent before the Lord?' the friend asked. And then she continued. 'So often I think that I am praying, but what I am actually doing is repeating my worries over and over to the Lord. Telling Him, "I don't want this," or "I can't do that"…minimizing all that He can do.'"[8] This shared wisdom caused Laura to commit to spending twenty minutes a day in God's presence, in silence. Instead of ruminating on her concerns or giving God instructions for how to better run the world, she's inviting Him to speak.

   B.  Create a list of places where you can go to hear from God. You might want to think about a nook in your house, a place to walk, or a certain park bench. Then make a list of the decisions you are currently facing. Finally, write a short prayer, asking the Holy Spirit to speak to you and guide you to the best choices.

   My designated discernment spaces:

   My current pending decisions:

---

8   Laura Phelps, "Here in the Nothingness," Walking with Purpose, February 2, 2021, https://walkingwithpurpose.com/here-in-the-nothingness/.

Dear Lord,

*Quiet your heart and enjoy His presence…He'll meet you in the silence.*

*As I reflect on my life, I realize it's almost always in the quiet that God has met me. It's at these times that I've received comfort in my suffering and clarity around decisions. Something I find interesting is this: If God has already told me something—if He has pointed out something I need to change—He waits to see how I respond to that word. If I decide it isn't to my liking and I ignore it, He waits. If I don't obey what He's asked of me, He waits for me at that place where I disregarded His words.*

*I'll rush forward, doing my own thing, and then wonder why He's so silent. That's when I realize I need to go back to the last time I felt Him speaking to me clearly. Did I do what He asked? And if I did it then, am I still obeying now, or have I gotten a little sloppy?*

*Another truth that's helped me as I seek to discern God's will: His voice does not contradict Scripture and teachings of the Church. He is not a God of confusion.*

*What's my point? I think we often say that we want to know God's will—we wish He would show up and tell us what to do, and He's whispering, "I already did."*

*Sometimes He speaks through Scripture. Sometimes it's through a faithful friend. Sometimes it's through a Church teaching. So, a good starting point is always checking out what He's already said. I think we all must admit that He's communicated quite a lot. But how have we responded to what He's said?*

# Day Three
## REJECT THE LIES

It would all be so much easier if the only voice in our heads was God's. But we have an enemy, and he is talking, too. We need to learn to recognize his voice and reject what he says. We're better equipped to do this when we know something of our enemy's tactics and nature.

1. A. How is our enemy described? See John 8:44 and Revelation 12:9.


   B. How does he disguise himself? See 2 Corinthians 11:14.


   C. Does the Church teach that this should all be interpreted as a metaphor, or is our enemy an actual being? What other insights do you gain into who we are up against? See CCC 391.


   D. Just before Jesus entered into His Passion, what did He say was going to happen? See John 12:31.


In his powerful book *Rescued*, Father John Riccardo sheds further insight on this passage:

> In identifying the enemy as "the ruler of this world," Jesus was not naively blaming evil on some supernatural power that doesn't exist. He was not an ignoramus who didn't know better, nor was he spouting outmoded, superstitious ways of thinking about Satan. Jesus dealt with concrete and eternal realities, and he called Satan "the ruler of this world." He spoke to us—and continues to speak through Scripture and the Church—about that third player on the stage, and we do well to listen to him…
>
> Many naively imagine that we were born into some sort of neutral territory, when in fact you and I were born in a war zone and into a battle. And the first step in surviving and then winning a war is knowing that you're at war.[9]

You are in the middle of a war zone, and many of the battles are won or lost *in your mind*. Your enemy is the third player on the stage, joining you and God. But make no mistake, "He who is in you [that's God Himself, through the indwelling Holy Spirit] is greater than he who is in the world" (1 John 4:4). A spiritual battle continues to rage, but we are assured that the victory belongs to Christ. That is not only the end of the story, it's our current reality. When Jesus died on the cross, He struck a death blow to the ruler of this

---

9    Father John Riccardo, *Rescued* (Frederick, MD: The Word Among Us, 2020), 67–8.

world. Our enemy is defeated, but he's got some skirmishes left in him. He continues to lie and deceive, but we can choose whether we listen to him.

2. What are we commanded to do in 2 Corinthians 10:5?

This excerpt from the Bible study *Fearless and Free* offers additional insight into this passage:

> What sort of empty arguments is Saint Paul talking about? We can recognize an empty argument when we see that it is pitting itself against what we know to be true about God. These arguments often make some degree of sense but are a twisting of the truth. They are a thin coating of reason that covers up a lie…
>
> The enemy was called a "false lover" by Saint Ignatius, because even as he entices us to look at things from his perspective instead of God's, even as he lures us with temptation, he wants to keep it a secret. In the words of Father Timothy Gallagher, "the enemy seeks to shroud his deceits…[but] our way of responding…will determine much of the subsequent course of the temptation, deception, or attack: whether these will diminish or increase their hold on us."[10] We are not victims of the enemy's deceits. We have a choice to either agree with his perspective or call him out on his lies. When we respond by asking ourselves, "Is this real or not real? Is this the truth or a lie?" we will significantly diminish the enemy's ability to mess with us.
>
> Taking every thought captive to Christ (2 Corinthians 10:5) means that we hear an argument (or lie) and immediately ask ourselves, "Is this true?" We challenge the argument or lie and compare it to what we read in Scripture and Church teachings.[11]

3. Read the following examples of lie-based thinking and circle the ones that often run through your mind. Then write out the lie that has the strongest hold on you. Next, cross it out. Finally, write the following beneath the crossed-out lie: That's a lie from the pit of hell.

---

10 Timothy M. Gallagher, *The Discernment of Spirits: An Ignatian Guide for Everyday Life* (New York: Crossroad, 2005), 150.

11 Lisa Brenninkmeyer, *Fearless and Free* (Walking with Purpose, 2019), 103–4.

I am all alone.
I can't do it.
Things will never change.
I am stuck.
I am defined by my failures.
My past controls my future.
Nobody understands me.
I am powerless.

It's all up to me.
I can't share my secret.
God doesn't love me.
God can't help me.
God doesn't care.
God isn't all-powerful.

The lie that runs through my mind most often:

(Be sure to cross it out!)

4.  To win the battle of the mind, it isn't enough to reject the lies that our enemy whispers. We need to replace the lies with truth. Read the following verses, noting what is true about God. Return to these verses often (underline them in your Bible), because the best way to counter a lie from the enemy is with a truth about the One who is all-powerful, all-loving, and ever victorious.

Deuteronomy 31:6

Psalm 46:1

Psalm 139:1

Jeremiah 29:11

Jeremiah 32:17

Lamentations 3:22–23

Malachi 3:6

Luke 1:37

1 Corinthians 10:13

Ephesians 2:4

1 John 1:9

*Quiet your heart and enjoy His presence...Rest in His promises.*

*A great way to start your morning is to get your thoughts down on paper, rather than letting them rumble around in your mind. The Walking with Purpose* Praying from the Heart: Guided Prayer Journal *is a great tool for this. It guides you through the process of getting your thoughts out, helping you identify any lie-based thinking, and then shifting focus to truths about God. The key is rejecting the lies and then replacing them with the truth of God's character and promises.*

*Dear God,*
*I acknowledge that a lot of my trouble comes from what is going on in my mind. This is where doubts swirl, judgments are made, fears take hold, and lies masquerade as truth. Help me to be disciplined with my time so that I begin my day in Your presence, paying careful attention to my thoughts. Help me to slow down and notice what is running through my head, instead of letting those thoughts run the show. Holy Spirit, help me to identify any lies, and to overcome my tendency to envisage the worse possible scenarios. When I stay locked in these destructive thought patterns, I am forgetting that Your presence turns even the hardest of circumstances into an opportunity for growth and greater closeness to You. I have the ability to choose what I think about. May my focus be on Your faithfulness and unfailing help. Amen.*

# Day Four
## REBOOT EACH MORNING

Tucked in the middle of the first Eucharistic prayer is the powerful petition, "order our days in your peace."[12] Isn't this what we want—to experience ordered, peace-filled

---

12  "Eucharistic Prayers I–IV," Catholic Resources (accessed February 2, 2021), https://www.catholic-resources.org/ChurchDocs/RM3-EP1-4.htm.

lives? If we want this to be our reality, we'd be wise to pay special attention to what we are allowing to fill the hours in our day, especially the earliest ones.

1.  How do you usually spend your morning? Describe your routine here:

2.  A.  Most of us have trouble being self-disciplined with our time. We may recognize that we waste a lot of it, but we aren't sure what to do about it. For some of us, demands on our time chase us relentlessly. We're purposeful about our time, but there's just too much to do. We can't catch up, no matter how hard we try. Although Jesus walked the earth thousands of years ago, He understands the temptation of distraction and how easy it is to fritter away time. He knows what it's like to lead a pressure-filled life, surrounded by never-ending needs. Yet Jesus never was robbed of interior peace, and He lived with perfect intentionality. Read Mark 1:35 and note the way Jesus started His day.

    B.  In Luke 3:4–6, John the Baptist is quoting the prophet Isaiah. What did "the voice of one crying in the wilderness" encourage his listeners to do?

        John the Baptist was begging his listeners to clear anything out of the way that was blocking the Lord from being close to them. His words weren't just meant for them—they are for you today.

What God desires is intimacy with you. He longs for you to clear the pathway to your heart so He can meet you there, offering you the strength and grace you need for the day ahead. God wants to help you with the ups and downs of life (described in Luke 3 as valleys, mountains, hills, and rough ways). He knows how they threaten your peace. God can be trusted to remove all obstacles and to smooth the rough ways when that is what is best for you. Your part is to clear the way in your schedule so that time with God isn't just a good intention, but the way that you start your day.

    C.  Are you taking time regularly *each day* to order your inner life? Does your day start with prayer? Why or why not?

3.   A.   What do you learn from the following verses about who and what should come first in your life?

Matthew 6:31–33

Colossians 1:15–18 (note that this passage is speaking of Jesus)

> Colossians 1:18 says that Christ is to be *preeminent* in everything, which means He is to have first place in all things. He wants to be first in our hearts, and we're also to give Him first place with our time.

This is one of those things that sound very good in theory and then prove difficult to live out. In his powerful book *The Way*, Saint Josemaría Escrivá insists that it's all about the first moment of the day. Seize it and you'll seize the day. Waste it and you're already behind the eight ball. He issues the following challenge:

> Conquer yourselves from the very first moment, getting up on the dot, at a set time, without granting a single minute to laziness. If, with the help of God, you conquer yourself in that moment, you'll have accomplished a great deal for the rest of the day. It's so discouraging to find yourself beaten in the first skirmish…

> The heroic minute. It's time to get up, on the dot! Without hesitation, a supernatural thought and…up! The heroic minute—here you have a mortification that strengthens your will and does not weaken your body.[13]

  B.   Which decisions and preparations could you make the night before in order to set your alarm and get up to pray first thing?

4.   In Day Three, we explored the importance of identifying the enemy's lies and replacing them with God's truth. This is the perfect way to start your day. How is this process described in Romans 12:2?

---

13   Josemaría Escrivá, *The Way* (New York: Doubleday, 1982), 31, 33.

The ideal morning reboot is one in which our minds are renewed. How do we renew our minds? We look at our thoughts, compare them to God's, dwell on the truths He has revealed, and reject what is false. When we do this, we are equipped to discern God's will and begin our day focused on the good. This isn't just an intellectual process; it's one that involves our whole self, mind and heart. This is a form of prayer that orders both the heart and the day.

I'd be remiss if I didn't say that there is no prayer more powerful than the Mass. It's my hope that you could meet Jesus in the Eucharist every day. So, the morning reboot I am describing here is not meant to replace the Mass, but to supplement it. This is a both/and proposition.

We all know how easy it is to mindlessly sit through Mass, never experiencing the renewal of our thoughts. We can check the "I went to Mass" box, and yet walk out the doors of the sanctuary with the same old destructive thoughts still in our heads. So, what I am describing is an intentional period of time (ideally first thing in the morning!) when we sit in God's presence, read His Word in Scripture, and ask for His perspective. We want to look at the world through the lens of Scripture, not look at Scripture through the lens of the world. Doing so requires setting time aside to delve in.

You might be wondering how to do this. Guess what. You already are. You are diving into Scripture with this Bible study as your guide. Another excellent resource is the *Praying from the Heart: Guided Prayer Journal*, which breaks down the process in greater detail.

*Quiet your heart and enjoy His presence…Get up at a set hour and stand amazed by the difference this makes.*

*If a battle wages in our minds each and every day, then we must pay attention to our private worlds. It's easier to put all our energy into the things that are public, and those are the activities that tend to earn us accolades and praise. But if we fail to order our private worlds, we'll later regret it. In the words of author and preacher Oswald Chambers, "The battle is lost or won in the secret places of the will before God, never first in the external world…Nothing has any power over [the person] who has fought out the battle before God and won there…I must get the thing settled between myself and God in the secret places of my soul where no stranger intermeddles, and then I can go forth with the certainty that the battle is won."[14]*

---

14   Oswald Chambers, "Where the Battle's Lost and Won," My Utmost for His Highest (accessed February 2, 2021), https://utmost.org/classic/where-the-battle's-lost-and-won-classic/.

*Dear Lord,*
*I want to offer You access to the secret place of my soul, where no stranger intermeddles. I want to hear Your voice, and I know You often speak in a whisper. Help me to budget time first thing in my day so I can turn to You for inner strength. Give me the gift of resolve and tenacity so that I can grab hold of that first heroic moment, pulling myself out of bed to meet with You. May I see this as a privilege, recognizing that I am being offered a private audience with the King of Kings, who is also the Lover of my soul. Amen.*

# Day Five
# RESPOND BY ABIDING

We began this lesson by exploring how to receive God's love, recognize His voice, reject the enemy's lies, and reboot each morning. Now we will sum it all up with one word: *abide.*

When we set out to make God the highest priority in our lives, we'll be tempted to strive to earn His love. But God's love can't be earned; it's meant to be received. That's what abiding is all about, and it's the key to living the Christian life victoriously.

*Abiding* describes a way of life. In the words of James Montgomery Boice, "When our Lord says: *Abide in me* he is talking about the will, about the choices, the decisions we make. We must decide to do things which expose ourselves to him and keep ourselves in contact with him. This is what it means to abide in him."[15]

**Read John 15:4–10.**

1.  A.  If our goal is fruitful living, what can we accomplish if we are disconnected from Christ? See John 15:4–5.

Apart from Christ we can do nothing? Then how do we explain the countless people who aren't Christians yet do a tremendous amount of good in the world? The key is understanding what Jesus meant when He said *bearing fruit.* Pastor David Guzik explains, "It isn't that the disciples could do no activity without Jesus. They could be active

---

15  James Montgomery Boice, *The Gospel of John*, vol. 4 (Grand Rapids, MI: Baker Books, 1999), 166–70.

without Him, as were the enemies of Jesus and many others. Yet they and we could do nothing of real, eternal value without Jesus."[16]

    B.  What does Jesus warn His disciples of in John 15:6?

2.  John 15:7–8 describes four things that happen when we abide in Christ and allow His words to abide in us. What are they?

These four things are all interconnected. Abiding in Christ should cause our very desires to be transformed so that the things we want are the things God wants for us. When we are pursuing what God wants, we bear fruit that is eternally significant. This glorifies God, and when people see us, they'll recognize Him in us.

3.  A.  We are commanded to abide in Christ's love. According to John 15:10, how do we do that?

    B.  Is there an area of your life where God has asked you to obey Him, but you are hesitating?

    C.  In CCC 787, we read of the intimate communion of love that Jesus invites us into. What do we learn from this passage about how to abide—how to experience communion—between His body and ours?

Again, these things are interconnected. We receive the strength to obey God through His love, given to us through the Eucharist. God doesn't ask us to obey Him in our

---

16  David Guzik, "John 15–The Departing Jesus Teaches His Disciples About Life in Him," Enduring Word (accessed February 3, 2021), https://enduringword.com/bible-commentary/john-15/.

own strength. He wants to infuse us with His, so we have everything we need to live the way He asks.

And how is He asking us to live? He's asking us to simplify our lives so they are focused on a few things that really matter.

4. Centering one's life around what matters most is something that monastic communities have understood for centuries. They were the first to develop a "rule of life," a schedule and practices that helped them abide in Christ. Author and pastor John Mark Comer writes of this in his excellent book, *The Ruthless Elimination of Hurry*:

> The word rule comes from the Latin word *regula*, which literally means "a straight piece of wood," (think: ruler), but it was also used for a trellis. Think of Jesus' teaching on abiding in the vine from John 15, one of the most important teachings on emotional health and spiritual life. Now think of a pleasant wine-tasting memory. What's underneath every thriving vine? A trellis. A structure to hold up the vine so it can grow and bear fruit…What a trellis is to a vine, a rule of life is to abide. It's a structure—in this case a schedule and a set of practices—to set up abiding as the central pursuit of your life…If a vine doesn't have a trellis, it will die. And if your life with Jesus doesn't have some kind of structure to facilitate health and growth, it will wither away. Following Jesus has to make it onto your schedule and into your practices or it will simply never happen.[17]

Three things will greatly enhance your time with Him: stillness, silence, and solitude. The following are good questions to help you discern if you are ready to construct a trellis for your life—a commitment to a schedule and practices that will help you abide in Christ.

Am I willing to disconnect from my phone and screens for a set period of time each day in order to sit in stillness with God?

Am I willing to turn off the noise and enter into silence so I can hear God's voice?

---

17    John Mark Comer, *The Ruthless Elimination of Hurry* (London, UK: Hodder & Stoughton, 2019), 95.

Will I designate a quiet place in my home where I can spend time in solitude? Will I vocalize my needs, asking loved ones to give me the gift of uninterrupted time?

"The reason we live in a culture increasingly without faith is not because science has somehow disproved the unprovable, but because the white noise of secularism has removed the very stillness in which it might endure or be reborn."[18] —Andrew Sullivan

*Quiet your heart and enjoy His presence…Stay with Him a little longer.*

*"For a few of us, abiding in Christ will be a mystical experience which is beyond words to express. For most of us, it will mean a constant contact with him. It will mean arranging life, arranging prayer, arranging silence in such a way that there is never a day when we give ourselves a chance to forget him."[19] —William Barclay*

*Dear Lord,*
*I want to abide in You. The word* abide *means to be present, to remain, to tarry, to endure.*

*Help me to be present with You, right now, in this moment. May I not regret the past nor fear the future. May I notice my thoughts and where they wander. Help me to bring them back to the present moment and focus on You.*

*Help me to remain with You, instead of following distractions. When I sit down to pray, all sorts of things start to vie for my attention. Help me to practice planned neglect. Help me to ignore them, knowing I will address them later.*

*Help me to tarry. Instead of rushing through my prayer time, may I take a deep breath, and just stay a few minutes longer than I'd planned. This is a kick in the teeth to the enemy and strengthens my will.*

*Help me to endure. The Christian life is not easy, and doubts often fill my mind. May I patiently endure circumstances that I don't understand. Instead of judging You by my circumstances, may I just judge my circumstances in the light of Your love and provision for me. May I endure the times when I don't have answers to my questions why. May I trust You with the unknown. Amen.*

---

18  Andrew Sullivan, "I Used to Be a Human Being," *New York*, September 19, 2016, https://nymag.com/intelligencer/2016/09/andrew-sullivan-my-distraction-sickness-and-yours.html.

19  William Barclay, *The Gospel of John*, vol. 2 (Louisville, KY: John Knox Press, 2017), 205.

# Conclusion

*"Abide with me; fast falls the eventide;*
*The darkness deepens; Lord with me abide;*
*When other helpers fail and comforts flee,*
*Help of the helpless, Oh, abide with me." —Henry Francis Lyte*

These words from the hymn "Abide with Me" are based on Luke 24:29, when the disciples on the road to Emmaus said to Jesus, "Stay with us, for it is toward evening and the day is now far spent." Jesus joined them at the dinner table, blessing and breaking the bread. And in that moment, their eyes were opened, and they realized who He was. But before they could grab hold of Jesus, He vanished from their sight. They had asked Him to stay. Why did He leave?

A deeper understanding of this passage makes it clear that Jesus answered their prayer. They recognized Him in the breaking of the bread, and it would be in the gift of Himself as the Bread of Life that He'd continue to stay. Jesus wanted to be intimately connected with His followers, so He made Himself small, a host, and offered Himself through the Eucharist.

There are times in life when God feels far away. We pray and don't sense His presence. What a gift it is to be able to receive Him physically as well as spiritually. Jesus promised us in Matthew 28:20, "Surely I am with you always, to the very end of the age." He has not left us alone. Psalm 138:3 says, "On the day I called, you answered me; You made me bold with strength in my soul." This is what happens when we receive the Eucharist and abide in Christ. He infuses our soul with His own strength, doing in and through us the very things that feel impossible.

I recently had one of those days when everything just felt exhausting. Staying faithful to God and my commitments felt like such an uphill climb. I reached out to a friend who understood what it is like to feel overwhelmed and like God just wasn't listening, like you were just left to languish on your own. She reminded me that this would not last forever. "This will end," she said. She reminded me that help would come and things would get better. She prayed that God would bless me with moments of refreshment so that I could take the next best step in my day. Even as she was typing those words, I had hauled myself to adoration. And that is the correct word for my action: *hauled*. I didn't feel like going. I wondered if it would make any difference. But it did. God refreshed my heart. No circumstances changed, but I received strength to carry on.

I wonder how your heart is doing today. What are you worried about? What are the unspoken needs and concerns that you carry? Does God feel close or distant? Do you feel alone? Let me assure you, there is not a detail of your life that Jesus does not care about. He is interested in everything that touches you.

Is it time to cancel some other commitments and to haul yourself to Jesus?

He is waiting for you.

*"Let us know, let us press on to know the LORD;*
*His going forth is as sure as the dawn;*
*He will come to us as the showers,*
*As the spring rains that water the earth." (Hosea 6:3)*

# My Resolution

"My Resolution" is your opportunity to write down one specific, personal application from this lesson. We can take in a lot of information from studying the Bible, but if we don't translate it into action, we have totally missed the point. In James 1:22, we're told that we shouldn't just hear the Word of God; we are to "do what it says." So what qualities should be found in a good resolution? It should be **personal** (use the pronouns *I, me, my, mine*), it should be **possible** (don't choose something so far-fetched that you'll just become discouraged), it should be **measurable** (a specific goal to achieve within a specific time period), and it should be **action oriented** (not just a spiritual thought).

Examples:

1. On Day Three, I recognized certain lies that often frequent my mind. I have read the verses that point me to the truths of God that counter those lies. I will write out the verse that stood out to me the most and put it various places to remind myself to replace the lie with the truth.

2. I want to experience the power of the heroic minute, getting up and giving God the first part of my day. I commit to doing that this week at this time: _____ and in this place: _____.

3. On Day Five, I acknowledged an area of my life where God has asked me to obey, but I have been hesitating to do so. I commit to doing what He has asked from this day forward (one day at a time), and will ask someone to hold me accountable with this commitment.

My Resolution:

## Catechism Clips

***CCC 391*** Behind the disobedient choice of our first parents lurks a seductive voice, opposed to God, which makes them fall into death out of envy. Scripture and the Church's Tradition see in this being a fallen angel, called "Satan" or the "devil." The Church teaches that Satan was at first a good angel, made by God: "The devil and the other demons were indeed created naturally good by God, but they became evil by their own doing."

***CCC 787*** From the beginning, Jesus associated his disciples with his own life, revealed the mystery of the Kingdom to them, and gave them a share in his mission, joy, and sufferings. Jesus spoke of a still more intimate communion between him and those who would follow him: "Abide in me, and I in you…I am the vine, you are the branches." And he proclaimed a mysterious and real communion between his own body and ours: "He who eats my flesh and drinks my blood abides in me, and I in him."

Looking for more material? We've got you covered! Walking with Purpose meets women where they are in their spiritual journey. From our Opening Your Heart 22-lesson foundational Bible study to more advanced studies, we have something to help each and every woman grow closer to Christ. Find out more:

www.walkingwithpurpose.com

# Lesson 3

# PRIORITY 2: YOUR HEART

## Introduction

You matter to God. All that you carry in your heart—your dreams, desires, needs, and heartaches—all this is seen by God. Far from being an impersonal deity who expects you to suck it up and soldier on, God pays attention to everything that touches you. In Psalm 56:9 David writes, "My wanderings you have noted; are my tears not stored in your flask, recorded in your book?" Let that sink in. The Creator of the Universe sees you, takes note of your every tear, and holds them. He keeps your tears. When you cry out to Him and say that you are at your limit, that you can't take any more, He sees everything that led up to that point. He sees it, and He cares. You are known and understood by God. You aren't too much for Him; you aren't too complicated; you aren't a mess in His eyes. He sees your beautiful, wild heart.

There is a deep longing found in the heart of women that has always existed. It's an interior restlessness, an ache for more. Whether or not we realize it, it's our longing for connection to God. But God is not the only one paying attention to the state of your heart and mine, or women's hearts in general. This has been a subject of interest and debate for some time. Betty Friedan wrote of it in *The Feminine Mystique* in the 1960s, describing it as "the problem that has no name."[20]

We have all seen the effects of a persuasive writer who is able to name what people are currently feeling but are unable to express. When someone nails it and artfully communicates what we've all been sensing and perceiving, powerful trends are born. Those trends translate into belief systems that are embraced and passed to the next generation. This is what happened with the writing of authors like Betty Friedan, Gloria Steinem, Kate Millett, and others. Their writing and influence birthed a movement that set out to heal the hearts of women by liberating them from the effects of patriarchy and

---

20  Betty Friedan, *The Feminine Mystique* (New York: W. W. Norton & Company, 2001), 433.

the chains of home life and motherhood. Decades later, it's worth asking: Are women happier as a result of their efforts? Statistics indicate they are not. Women have never been more medicated, addicted, and confused.

This mission to liberate women has been picked up by women in each subsequent generation, and writers and influencers continue to persuasively describe women's current feelings. Women read these books, blogs, and social media posts and think, *Yes. That's me. She sees me. She understands me. She's putting into words what I've not been able to name.* Influencers tap into women's discontent, articulate what women are feeling, and then offer solutions.

A No. 1 *New York Times* best seller that has sold millions of copies and is considered a book packed with wisdom for women today offers this solution:

> We do not need more selfless women. What we need right now is more women who have detoxed themselves so completely from the world's expectations that they are full of nothing but themselves. What we need are women who are *full of themselves*. A woman who is full of herself knows and trusts herself enough to say and do what must be done. She lets the rest burn.[21]

In years past, I have enjoyed this author's personality, sense of humor, authenticity, and vulnerability. She has raised millions of dollars for people in need and I commend her for it. But I pause and am deeply concerned with the direction in which her writing is going. We need more women who are *full of themselves*? I don't think so.

You are being delivered a steady message through the media regarding the best way to care for yourself. Self-care represents a $10 billion per year industry in the United States.[22] Make no mistake, there is vested interest in getting you to care for your heart in such a way that keeps the economic engine running. But is it possible that you are being offered counterfeit self-care? Could it be that the bill of goods we've been sold for decades isn't delivering on its promises? Might it be that the very things that we are "letting burn" are the things that we most need in order to be fulfilled?

Are you ready to allow the Creator of your heart to show you what will truly satisfy your deepest longings? Let's explore *true* self-care, the kind that satisfies our yearning to know who we are and what we are worth.

---

21  Glennon Doyle, *Untamed* (New York: Dial Press, 2020), 75.

22  Alice Hickson and Lilly Blumenthal, "The Self Care Obsession," March 25, 2019, *Tufts Observer*, https://tuftsobserver.org/the-self-care-obsession/.

# Day One
## TRUE SELF-CARE: CONNECT TO YOUR HEART

*"The internal voice that tells me to hustle can find a to-do list in my living room as easily as it can in an office…And I know that activity—any activity—keeps me from feeling, so that becomes a drug, too. I'll run circles around this house, folding clothes and closing cabinets, sweeping and tending to things, never allowing myself to feel the cavernous ache. Which brings us, literally, to the heart of the conversation: the heart, the cavernous ache. Am I loved? Does someone see me? Do I matter? Am I safe?"[23] —Shauna Niequist*

1. Does the quote from Shauna Niequist resonate with you? Why or why not? Do you find that increased activity and hustle in your life causes you to avoid connecting with what you are feeling? *To the point of annoyance because it exacerbates the ache of 'Do I matter'*

2. The word *heart* is used in many different ways. In order to center our study around a common definition, read the following Bible verses, and note what the Bible says about the heart.

    Matthew 9:4 *Thoughts are linked to heart. 'Thoughts of the heart'*

    John 16:22 *Heart contains emotions 'Hearts will be full of joy'*

    Acts 11:23 (NABRE version) *Hearts can be full of purpose. (will)*

    Hebrews 10:22 *Heart that is full of faith & sincerity (conscience)*

Putting these verses together, we learn that our hearts contain our thoughts, emotions, will, and conscience.

---

23  Shauna Niequist, *Present Over Perfect* (Grand Rapids, MI: Zondervan, 2016), 37.

3. Read the way the heart is described in CCC 2563 and fill in the missing words.

**CCC 2563** The heart is the dwelling-place where I am, where I live; according to the Semitic or Biblical expression, the heart is the place "to which I withdraw." The heart is our _our hidden center_, beyond the grasp of our reason and of others; only the _Spirit of God_ _____ can fathom the human heart and know it fully. The heart is the place of _decision_____, deeper than our psychic drives. It is the place of truth, where we choose life or death. It is the place of _encounter_____, because as image of God we live in _relation_____: it is the place of covenant.

4. CCC 2563 says that our heart, "our hidden center, [is] beyond the grasp of our reason and of others." What additional insight into this do you gain from Jeremiah 17:9?

*Heart is deceitful.*

This verse is not intended to spiral us down a path of self-loathing. But it reveals something very important: our hearts can deceive us. One problem is our seemingly limitless ability to rationalize our behavior. Another is our tendency to self-protect.

We all have experienced being deeply hurt, even traumatized. In those moments, our heart's core questions (Am I loved? Does someone see me? Do I matter? Am I safe?) were answered with a resounding *no*. When this happened, we instinctively responded in a certain way, whether we were aware of it or not. We experienced the trauma and were down on the mat. At this time, the enemy whispered lies to us. These lies sounded like truth in the moment. He spoke (and continues to speak) lies like, "You are all alone." "You are powerless." "You will never recover from this." "You are ruined." "This happened to you because you are a bad person." "You must never speak of this."

These thoughts run through our minds without our even being aware of their source. And the normal response is to resolve to never get ourselves into a situation like this again. We make a vow to protect ourselves. What we don't realize is that we've agreed with a lie and are now making a decision to behave in a certain way going forward. God has not been invited into the situation to heal us, and as a result, a wound forms.

What is my point? God must be invited to speak truth into our hearts. "Only the Spirit of God can fathom the human heart and know it fully" (CCC 2563). When we invite Him into our hidden center and ask Him to speak truth to our brokenness, He always comes. This encounter is sacred, powerful, and transformative.

I encourage you to invite Him into your painful memories, and ask Him to shed light on what is true so that you can reject the lies that hold you back. The following testimony explains the difference this can make:

> People who have been healed by a personal experience of Jesus entering their painful memories report freedom, no more need to judge those involved, and most profoundly, a knowing that what they now see about themselves and the situation is unquestionably, profoundly and peacefully true. True knowing comes to the heart that sees and hears "God with us."[24]

I have experienced this myself, and words fail to describe the way in which something that was once too painful to remember is now transformed into a deeper awareness of the truth that God has never left me.

But I admit, I wasn't able to go through this process of healing without help. Experienced intercessory prayer, counseling, and time learning from Dr. Bob Schuchts of the John Paul II Healing Center were all game changers. It is beyond the scope of this Bible study to fully explain the process, but I encourage you to seek out this kind of help. It could be the key to unlocking the interior freedom you so desire. I wrote the Bible study *Fearless and Free* to delve deeper into this pursuit of healing and wholeness and recommend it as a follow-up to this study.

5. What does Psalm 51:6 say that God desires for us? What does the psalmist ask God for in the second part of the verse? Personalize this verse, turning it into a prayer.

*Behold, you delight in truth in the inward being, and you teach me wisdom in the secret heart.*

*God, help me to hold your truth in my heart to gain wisdom deep within.*

---

24  James G. Freisen et al., *The Life Model: Living from the Heart Jesus Gave You* (East Peoria, IL: Shepherd's House, 2013), 144.

*Quiet your heart and enjoy His presence…"Draw near to God and He will draw near to you" (James 4:8).*

*If we are going to live intentionally and thrive, it will be critical for us to take time each day to put down the to-do list and connect with our hearts. This will require withdrawing from noise and people, and inviting God into this encounter.*

*When we move into this place of quiet reflection, we can ask Him to teach us—to shed light on what we are feeling and ask Him to speak wisdom into any confusion or pain we may be experiencing. This is a critical step if we want to be women who walk in truth. Doing this unites our hearts with His.*

*We can't figure ourselves out without His help. Trying to do so leaves us frustrated and often wandering down a path that leads to a bigger mess. Only the Spirit of God can see things with utter clarity. We desperately need His wisdom and perspective.*

*Dear Lord,*
*Here is my heart. I ask You to encounter me here, in this hidden place where my decisions are made. I'm tempted to make decisions based on my feelings. But because I know my heart and feelings can mislead me, I am inviting You in, and asking You to shed light on what is true.*

*My heart longs for answers to these questions…*
*Am I loved?*
*Do You see me?*
*Do I matter?*

*Am I safe?*

*I pause, and listen to Your voice say:*

*"I have loved you with an everlasting love; therefore I have continued my faithfulness to you." (Jeremiah 31:3)*
*"The LORD sees not as man sees; man looks on the outward appearance, but the lord looks on the heart." (1 Samuel 16:7)*
*"You are precious in my eyes, and honored, and I love you." (Isaiah 43:4)*
*"In peace I will both lie down and sleep; for you alone, O LORD, make me dwell in safety." (Psalm 4:8)*

*I hear You, Lord. I rebuke the lies and recognize their source. I receive Your words as truth. Amen.*

# Day Two
## TRUE SELF-CARE: KNOW YOUR WORTH

*"The human being is single, unique, and unrepeatable, someone thought of and chosen from eternity, and someone called and identified by name."*[25] *—Saint John Paul II "Urbi et Orbi," Christmas 1978*

1.  How would you answer the question "Who am I?" Do you change who you are depending on who you are with? Do you ever feel you wear masks so often that you aren't sure who you really are underneath it all?

    *Sometimes – I wish we all could be transparent + authentic.*

Those questions have to do with identity. It's our tendency to answer with a list of our roles. We might say…

I'm an athlete.
I'm a mother.
I'm a student.
I'm a single woman.
I'm an actress.
I'm a lawyer.
I'm a creative.
I'm a wife.

But God says that your true identity is something that can never be taken away. That means a role is not a true identity, because roles can change. They can't be counted on.

Perhaps you answered with words like…

I'm a mess.
I'm ugly.
I'm unwanted.
I'm stupid.
I'm boring.
I'm alone.
I'm untalented.
I can't do anything right.

---

25  John Paul II, "Urbi et Orbi: Message of His Holiness John Paul II, Christmas 1978," December 25, 1978, https://www.vatican.va/content/john-paul-ii/en/messages/urbi/documents/hf_jp-ii_mes_19781225_urbi.html.

I'm too fat.
I'm powerless.
I'm rejected.

My friend, that is *not* who you are. Those self-defeating thoughts are a litany of lies that need to be rejected outright.

2. A. What does God say about who you are? Read the following verses and record any insights into how God sees you.

Psalm 103:12 *I am forgiven – my transgression are as far as the east is from the west.*

Isaiah 43:1 *I am His – He has called you by name*

John 15:16 *I am chosen*

1 Corinthians 8:3 *I am known by God*

Ephesians 1:4–6 *I am not alone. I am God's beloved daughter.*

B. In the words of Saint John Paul II:

It is Jesus that you seek when you dream of happiness; He is waiting for you when nothing else you find satisfies you; He is the beauty to which you are so attracted; it is He who provoked you with that thirst that will not let you settle for compromise; it is He who urges you to shed the masks of a false life.[26]

Is there a mask you need to shed in order to grab hold of your true identity as a daughter of God? (Examples of masks: the cool girl, the humorist, the martyr, the overachiever, the bully, the control freak, the self-basher, the people pleaser, the introvert, the social butterfly…[27])

---

26  John Paul II, "15th World Youth Day, Address of the Holy Father John Paul II," August 19, 2000, http://www.vatican.va/content/john-paul-ii/en/speeches/2000/jul-sep/documents/hf_jp-ii_spe_20000819_gmg-veglia.html.

27  Therese J. Borchard, "The 10 Masks We Wear," PsychCentral, February 17, 2019, https://psychcentral.com/blog/the-10-masks-we-wear#5.

3.  A.  Where does our inherent dignity come from? See Genesis 1:26 and CCC 1700.

*Our inherent dignity is in the image ~~of Christ~~ & likeness of God.*

B.  How do we wound our dignity? See CCC 1487.

*When we sin, we wound our dignity*

CCC 2736 says that "the dignity of [God's] children lies in their freedom." We are free to make choices that promote our dignity or wound it, but we can never remove it from ourselves. Our dignity is a gift given to each one of us by our Creator. There is nothing we can do that takes away our intrinsic worth.

4.  A.  One of the ways we reflect the image and likeness of God is in our ability to give of self. This is our greatest calling, and it is utterly countercultural. The culture around us delivers the message that the key to finding fulfillment is putting yourself first. Jesus said the opposite in Matthew 16:25. Put this verse into your own words.

*Whoever wants to save their life will lose it but if we lose our life for God, will find eternal life with God. As christians, we shouldn't worry about this life.*

B.  Is there an area of your life where you are being called to give of yourself sacrificially? Has the hidden nature of that service caused you to question whether it's worth your time or really matters? In what way does God's perspective on the value of self-giving change your outlook?

*I wish I would prioritize the gift of self-giving instead of giving into the worldly + numerous reasons why I can't or maybe later... what am I waiting for? And what am I teaching my children about self-giving.*

*Quiet your heart and enjoy His presence…May He infuse you with divine love.*

*"At the core of every woman's heart—though it may be buried under abuse, contempt, ignorance, or misunderstanding—is the desire to be fruitful, to be a vessel, spiritually and physically, for others to find strength, care, affirmation, charity, nurturing, and home. Fertility is the desire to do good things. Edith Stein said that women 'fulfill themselves by giving something of their own life so that others may live.'"[28] —Carrie Gress*

*Giving of self is critical if we want to experience a satisfying life. There is a harmful cultural message delivered to women that suggests that a life of self-sacrifice through motherhood or caring for others is less valuable than one marked by productivity and achievement. This has caused our society to devalue what Saint John Paul II described as the feminine genius, our unique ability to create room for the other—to see people and their value not because of what they do, but for who they are.*

*Do you recognize these traps laid for women in our society?*

- *failing to value what makes women unique, and instead encouraging them to act like men (often emulating their worst traits)*
- *looking at motherhood as what holds women back from achieving their true potential*
- *looking at women serving their families and others as somehow "less than"*

*We bring the heart, the nurturing, the empathy, the receptivity, and the focus on the primacy of love. And this is essential to building a flourishing society. We are more than consumers and producers. We are relational beings at the core, and if we as women neglect our gifts, our families and communities will disintegrate.*

*It is time for women to see who they truly are, allowing the One who created them to define their worth. It is time for women to shed the masks and offer people authentic relationships—soft places to land. It is time for us to value self-sacrifice over productivity and achievement. It is time for us to embrace our feminine genius and be a part of bringing healing and wholeness to the world.*

*There is no greater example of the feminine genius than the Blessed Mother. Turn to her now with your needs. She'll go to her son on your behalf. Do you need God the Father to speak your true identity into the depths of your soul? This is a gift He longs to give you.*

*The Memorare*

*Remember, O most gracious Virgin Mary,*
*That never was it known*

---

28  Carrie Gress, *The Anti-Mary Exposed: Rescuing the Culture from Toxic Femininity* (Charlotte, NC: Tan Books, 2019), 134.

*That anyone who fled to thy protection,*
*Implored thy help, or sought thy intercession*
*Was left unaided.*
*Inspired by this confidence, I fly unto thee,*
*O Virgin of virgins, my mother; to thee do I come,*
*Before thee I stand, sinful and sorrowful.*
*O Mother of the Word Incarnate, despise not my*
*Petitions, but in thy mercy hear and answer me.*
*Amen.*

## Day Three
## TRUE SELF-CARE: CULTIVATE AN UNHURRIED LIFE

*"A 'successful' life has become a violent enterprise. We make war on our own bodies, pushing them beyond their limits; war on our children, because we cannot find enough time to be with them when they are hurt and afraid and need our company; war on our spirit, because we are too preoccupied to listen to the quiet voices that seek to nourish and refresh us; war on our communities, because we are fearfully protecting what we have, and do not feel safe enough to be kind and generous; war on the earth, because we cannot take the time to place our feet on the ground and allow it to feed us, to taste its blessings and give thanks."[29]* —Wayne Muller

1.  A.  Circle the following statement(s) that best express how you feel about your pace of life:

> ✓ I can't catch my breath. I have no margin.
> ✓ Anxiety is always simmering below the surface.
> I have time in the day to do what matters most to me and usually end my day feeling satisfied.
> ✓ Too often, people feel like interruptions because my schedule is maxed out.
> ✓ I'm on the verge of emotional burnout.
> I move at a slow-enough pace to notice when the people around me need my care and concern, and I am able to stop and give them time.
> ✓ I'm easily irritated because of an underlying sense of being utterly overwhelmed.

---

29  Wayne Muller, *Sabbath: Finding Rest, Renewal, and Delight in Our Busy Lives* (New York: Bantam, 1999), 2.

B. If you could change one thing about your pace of life, what would it be?

*Slow down and learn how to take time to appreciate the smallest of things as true gifts or blessings.*

C. Which barriers prevent you from making that change?

*There always seems to be something to do, expectations to be met*

2. A. What wisdom can we glean from Ecclesiastes 3:1–8 that can help us to lead less hurried lives? *For everything there is a season. We aren't meant to do everything all at once*

B. Are you trying to do something in your current season of life that would be better done in a later season? *Outside of my marriage, my faith and my family - everything else should take a back seat but so often it's the opposite*

3. A. Which area of our lives do Psalm 101:3 and 119:37 address? What instruction is given to us? *We are told to not put anything that is worthless or wicked in our eyes and to turn away from all vanities.*

Our private lives drastically changed in 2007, the year the iPhone came on the market. According to a 2016 study, most of us tap, touch, and swipe our phone screens 2,617 times a day and spend about two and a half hours with our eyes glued to them.[30] We may feel we are utterly in control and able to put our phones down easily, but the data out there suggests otherwise. As statistician and Yale professor Edward Tufte stated in the powerful documentary *The Social Dilemma*, "There are only two industries that call their customers 'users': illegal drugs and software."[31] Research shows that social media has mastered the art of guiding us to behaviors that release dopamine (the "feel-good" chemical) in our brains. Each time we get a like, a comment, or a notification, we get a hit. Like it or not, this is addictive. We are less in control than we think.

---

30  Julia Naftulin, "Here's How Many Times We Touch Our Phones Every Day," *Business Insider*, July 13, 2016, https://finance.yahoo.com/news/research-shows-touch-cell-phones-142700933.html.

31  Emily White, "Six Chilling Quotes from 'The Social Dilemma,'" November 23, 2020, *The Utah Statesman*, https://usustatesman.com/six-chilling-quotes-from-the-social-dilemma/#:~:text=Six%20chilling%20quotes%20from%20'The%20Social%20Dilemma'%201,a%20curse."%20—%20Sophocles.%20...%20More%20items...%20.

B. What are we encouraged to do in Ephesians 5:15–16?

*We are told to look carefully - make the most of our time*

These verses challenge us to live our lives with purpose and conviction, discerning what's a good use of our time and using it wisely. Our days are filled with many things we genuinely need to do, but we fritter away a lot of time on distractions.

C. Are there any changes you could make in terms of screen time in order to slow down and be more present?

*Simply lock it up & put it away.*

"Do not let your phone set your emotional equilibrium and your news feed set your view of the world…Our morning news feed is not an accurate picture of the world. It is curated, not only with a sociopolitical agenda that is thoroughly secular (on both the left and the right) but also with an eye to all that is evil in the world, rarely to any of what is good. Because bad news is where the money is."[32] —John Mark Comer

4. A. What commandment did God give us to help us overcome our tendency toward rushing past instead of truly living our lives? See Exodus 20:8–11.

*Remember the Sabbath day & keep it holy. We are to rest on the 7th day - No work.*

B. Read the other commandments in Exodus 20:3–17, inserting your name before each one. Do you notice that you tend to take some more seriously than others? Why do you think we so quickly disregard the Sabbath rest God commands us to take?

*Because we haven't learned to balance our lives properly. We have prioritized busy-ness and work as some sign of worth + achievement. I wonder what it would look + feel like to truly rest on the sabbath. I imagine that it might just transform us as individuals and as a family.*

32 Comer, *The Ruthless Elimination of Hurry*, 228–9.

C. The Sabbath provides a wonderful opportunity to set aside one day a week for countercultural living. It's a day to do the things that delight you and bring refreshment. It's a day for being instead of doing. What are some things you would look forward to if you scheduled them for Sunday? What might change if you had a technology-free day on Sunday and gave your eyes a rest?

*might interact more with the kids on a deeper, more meaningful level.*

*Quiet your heart and enjoy His presence…Jesus is not in a hurry.*

*A great crowd was surrounding Jesus when suddenly a ruler of the synagogue, Jairus, came and fell at His feet. He looked up at Jesus and begged, "My little daughter is at the point of death. Come and lay your hands on her, so that she may be made well, and live" (Mark 5:23). Jesus immediately went with him.*

*In that same crowd was a woman, walking quickly with her head bent down. Being so close to so many people was risky. This woman had been deeply suffering for twelve years from a flow of blood. Mark 5:26 reveals that she was suffering physically (doctors couldn't find a cure), financially (she had spent all she had), and spiritually (the blood flow meant she was unclean and not allowed in the temple). The woman came up behind Jesus, not wanting to be seen. With a heart full of faith, she reached out her hand and touched the Healer. "Immediately the hemorrhage ceased; and she felt in her body that she was healed of her disease" (Mark 5:29).*

*One would think that would have been the end of it. That in the press of the crowd, Jesus would continue to Jairus' home and the woman would quietly move on. Jesus had important things to do. A child was dying. And not just any child—the child of an important, influential leader. But Jesus stopped and turned around. "Who touched me?" He said.*

*"Who touched you?" the disciples asked. They looked around at the crowd and pointed out that it could have been any of a number of people. Loads of people were touching Jesus. Who knew which hand had reached out? They needed to keep moving. There were more important things to tend to. But Jesus' eyes scanned the crowd. He looked around to see who had done it.*

*The woman stepped forward in fear and trembling and fell down before Him. Jesus didn't condemn her. In fact, there must have been something in His eyes, something in the way that He looked at her, that made time stand still. Because the woman at His feet "told him the whole truth" (Mark 5:33). It all came spilling out—all the hurt, the rejection, the loss, the pain, the fear, the ache, the longing; she poured out her heart to Him. And He listened. He saw her. In that moment, He made sure she knew that she mattered. He said to her, "Daughter"—and this was the only time Jesus ever used that term of endearment—"your faith has made you well; go in peace and be healed of your disease" (Mark 5:34).*

*Jesus was never so hurried that He missed the important. Urgent things vied for His attention, but He was always able to pause and tend to what was critical. This is how He tends to you. And this is the example He sets for you. His words to the first disciples are His words to you: "Follow me" (Matthew 4:19). Who are you tempted to hurry past? Can you ask God to give you His perspective so that you not only notice the people it's easy to rush by but also have the patience to stop long enough to look in their eyes?*

## Day Four
## TRUE SELF-CARE: TREAT YOUR BODY AS A TEMPLE OF THE HOLY SPIRIT

We live in a culture obsessed with outward appearance. When we think about our bodies, we likely first think about matters of beauty, weight, or fitness. What is the right perspective?

1. What do you learn about your body from Genesis 1:26 (the first part of the verse)?

   *We were made in His image & likeness*

2. A. What do you learn about your body from 1 Corinthians 6:19–20?

   *Our body is the temple of the Holy Spirit.*

   B. According to these verses, is your body your own, to do with as you please?

   *No, our body is but a temple — therefore we should be honoring God with our body (+ spirit)*

At the time of the early Church, the Christian perspective on the body was in direct opposition to the reigning cultural view. The Greco-Roman worldview was rooted in platonic thinking. Plato taught that the body was a prison, something that you'd finally be liberated from through death.[33] With that perspective, it was acceptable to use your body as a pleasure machine because all that really mattered was the here and now. This led to sexual acts that we consider illegal and abhorrent being acceptable and even celebrated in their culture.[34]

---

[33] "What Did Plato Think About Human Nature?" Reference, March 25, 2020, https://www.reference.com/world-view/did-plato-think-human-nature-95917f844717fe3d.

[34] Jenna Ross, "Pedophilia in Ancient Greece and Rome," May 23, 2020, The Collector, https://www.thecollector.com/pedophilia-ancient-greece-rome/.

Against that backdrop, Christian sexual ethics and the Christian view of the body were totally countercultural. Far from considering the Christian approach to be repressive or backward, women at that time found it incredibly liberating. The culture had been feeding them the message that what you do with your body doesn't matter. But their bodies had stored trauma, shame, and pain. Even as women were told that these things don't matter, especially if they were their own choices, their bodies said otherwise.

Saint Paul spoke into this mess and cast a vision far greater than what was being offered by the culture. The culture said that people were free to pursue whatever sexual expression they liked, that their bodies didn't matter. Saint Paul's vision was an elevated one: not only does your body matter, *your body houses the Spirit of God.*

3. Read the following verses and reflect on how you are treating your body.

  A. Psalm 127:2 *In vain you Rise early & stay up late toiling for food to eat — for he grants sleep to those he loves*

  Are you getting enough rest?
  *When I listen to my body.*

  B. Philippians 4:8 *Think about such things: True, Noble, Right, Pure, Lovely, admirable, excellent, praiseworthy*

  What are you putting in your mind? What are you dwelling on?
  *Spending too much time thinking on dwelling on unimportant things*

  C. 1 Corinthians 9:24–27
  *Need for self-discipline. Strict training for the crown of eternal life.*

  Are you training your body for the marathon of a life spent serving God? Are you exercising and eating well so your body has the energy it needs? Are you drinking enough water?

  D. Ephesians 5:18 *Do not get drunk on wine, which leads to debauchery. Instead, be filled with the Spirit*

Are you asking God to release the fullness of the Holy Spirit within you, or are you instead turning to alcohol to numb the ache? Do you think your drinking patterns might be a cause for concern?

4.  Take an inventory of your body and the way it serves you. Think of the parts of your body, not measuring them against cultural ideals, but instead with a spirit of thankfulness as you note the many ways your body does hard things. Note the things your body does that spread more love in our world.

*your purpose is to know God and love Him*

*Quiet your heart and enjoy His presence…Because "if anyone is in Christ, he is a new creation; the old has passed away, behold, the new has come" (2 Corinthians 5:17).*

*"A new heart I will give you, and a new spirit I will put within you." (Ezekiel 36:26)*

*An incredible thing happens when the Holy Spirit comes and makes His home in your soul. He makes you new. He transforms you from the inside out. He does the work within you of helping you become the truest version of yourself—that of a beloved daughter of God. He infuses you with purpose and power. This is the story of what happens when our lives intersect the love of Jesus.*

*What other stories have you heard? Have you listened to the story our world tells about why you are here? It delivers the message that you are the product of chance, of cells randomly coming together. You enter the world without a transcendent purpose. Because there is no overarching narrative—nothing that makes sense of the suffering and evil in the world—there is also no universal meaning. It is up to you to figure out who you are, what your purpose is, and the meaning of it all.*

*Do you know what that secular story results in? Anxious people. People who are overwhelmed by the burden of choice—by the need to figure things out and make decisions. Identity, purpose, meaning—these are things people feverishly try to discover and create, when all the while, God has offered them as a gift.*

*The true story is that you were dreamed up by God the Father even before you were conceived in your mother's womb. You are His chosen, precious child. Your purpose is to know God and love Him. Your life has tremendous meaning. Thomas Merton writes of this in his book* New Seeds of Contemplation:

*Next book:*
*A Tree grows in Brooklyn*

*The secret of my identity is hidden in the love and mercy of God...Therefore, I cannot hope to find myself anywhere except in him...Therefore there is only one problem on which all my existence, my peace, and my happiness depend: to discover myself in discovering God. If I find him, I will find myself, and if I find my true self, I will find him.[35]*

*Jesus loves you so much and has never wanted you to feel alone. That's why He spoke the words of John 14:16–18: "And I will ask the Father, and he will give you another Counselor, to be with you forever, even the Spirit of truth, whom the world cannot receive, because it neither sees him nor knows him; you know him, for he dwells with you, and will be in you. I will not leave you desolate. I will come to you."*

*Ask the Holy Spirit to guide you closer to God. Ask Him to help you see yourself and discover your true identity and purpose in the heart of the Father.*

## Day Five
## TRUE SELF-CARE: ACTIVELY PURSUE MATURITY

Maturity helps us *respond* to whatever intersects our path rather than just *react* to it. It helps us develop grit and resilience while still keeping our hearts soft. So often we feel we are faced with two alternatives: going to pieces emotionally when hardship strikes or just gritting our teeth and getting through it. Maturity opens up a third possibility: taking the time to open our hearts to what God is trying to teach us in this moment and remaining aware of what our hearts are feeling. This heightened awareness helps us to recognize and reject the enemy's lies.

1.  In 1 Corinthians 14:20, we read about an area of our lives that should be mature. What is it? How is the opposite of maturity described?

    *In our thinking - mature*
    *with respect to evil - be like infants*

2.  Is spiritual maturity guaranteed with age? See CCC 1308. Summarize the key teaching point that the Catechism makes here.

    *No, it is not guaranteed.*
    *spiritual maturity can come at any age regardless*
    *of life experience*

3.  How is a mature Christian described in Colossians 1:9–10?

    *A person filled with the knowledge*
    *of God's will.*

---

35 Thomas Merton, *New Seeds of Contemplation* (New York: New Directions, 2007), 35–6.

*spiritual wisdom + understanding and uses*
*what one knows to lead a life worthy of the Lord,*
*fully pleasing to Him, bearing fruit in every good*
*work and increasing in knowledge of God*

In the words of author Elisabeth Elliot, "The will of God is not something you add to your life. It's a course you choose. You either line yourself up with the Son of God…or you capitulate to the principle which governs the rest of the world."[36]

A mature woman filters everything she is experiencing through the lens of God's will. She's pursuing growth. She's teachable. She also is growing day by day in her ability to recognize and accept that whatever intersects her life has first passed through God's hands. He has allowed it because He has already figured out how to bring good from it, no matter how much evidence points to the contrary. She doesn't just *get* through it; she *grows* through it. This is true self-care, because it settles her heart and helps her look forward with hope.

4. I would be remiss if I didn't acknowledge that some of us were given a better foundation for the development of maturity than others. It's been said that the two greatest blocks to maturity are unfinished trauma recovery and the lack of life-giving relationships.[37] Can you identify any areas in your own life where you can see your maturity is blocked because of either of these things?

*I have been very fortunate in this regard — it is my own laziness + pride that blocks my maturity.*

Here's the good news. "If there is a shortfall in maturity, people can catch up, through their own willingness, with help from others, and by the power of God. You can create a better life for yourself and for others."[38]

If you want to further explore the role of healing in the journey toward maturity, I recommend the book *The Life Model: Living from the Heart Jesus Gave You.* The authors provide practical help, guideposts to gauge your own maturity level, and the assurance that your dignity and value do not increase or decrease depending on your maturity. It's an important and worthy pursuit, but God doesn't love mature women more than those who are really needing to grow in this area. His love is unconditional. Always.

---

36 Joe Reciniello, Catholic365, March 22, 2019, https://www.catholic365.com/article/10028/the-will-of-god-is-not-something-you-add-to-your-life-its-a-course-you-choose-you-either-line-yourself-up-with-the-son-of-godor-you-capitulate-to-the.html.

37 Freisen et al., *The Life Model*, 48.

38 Freisen et al., *The Life Model*, 52.

*Quiet your heart and enjoy His presence…You are His beloved child.*

*While I believe wholeheartedly in the importance of seeking healing and unity in our families, there are times when we simply cannot get what we need from a family member. Sometimes the best that a person is able to offer us still falls short of what we need. When this is the case, the family of God can make a tremendous difference in our ability to move past blockages to our maturity and grow up on the soul level.*

*One of our most basic needs is to belong. God invites us into a familial relationship and promises to be a good Father. Jesus is our protective big brother; there is nothing He won't do to save us. Our heavenly mother prays for us, going to God on our behalf, asking for what we need. We belong to a healthy spiritual family.*

*But God knows that there are times you need to see someone with your own eyes. You need an actual hug. You might need someone to remind you of who you really are, or teach you practical life skills, or hold you accountable, or mentor you. It's wonderful when the people who provide those things for us belong to our biological families. But when that's not been our experience, we can form intentional relationships with mature members of our community who are willing to fill in that gap.*

*Dear God,*
*Thank You for helping me to figure out what my heart needs. I'm grateful that You are a good Father who sees the things I've gone through and why my maturity has been blocked at times. Help me to do the work of honestly assessing places where I need to grow. Lead me to people who can fill in any relational gaps that I have experienced. Stay with me when I delve into areas of my heart that are painful to visit.*

*I want to follow Your will for my life—I don't want my thinking or my reactions to difficulty to be childish. So Holy Spirit, come. Be my guide, be my strength, be my advocate. Help my soul to grow. Amen.*

# Conclusion

Our lives will never be perfect this side of heaven. Accepting imperfection and knowing when good is good enough is critical for mental health. It's healthy and wise to recognize our own brokenness. Choosing to be authentic rather than wearing a mask of "I'm fine" or "I've got it all together" is also good for the heart. But is it possible that in our pursuit of authenticity, we can fall into the trap of becoming content with being less than who God created us to be? If we are practicing a form of self-care that gives us permission to remain immature in our thinking and behavior, we are doing ourselves a disservice.

Author Josh Meyers explores this topic in his article "Have We Made Authenticity an Idol?" He expresses concern that *authenticity* has become a Christian buzzword, and that "we've fallen for the fallacy that authenticity is the goal rather than the means God uses to achieve his real goal for our lives on earth,"[39] which is growing in holiness. Why do we fall into this trap? Because it's easier to be authentic than to do the work of growing in spiritual maturity. Meyers challenges his readers to pursue authenticity as a means to an end. The end is recognizing the ways in which we fall short, confessing our sin, and asking for God's help to live differently. This is what will bring the kind of interior transformation we long for.

The Blessed Mother offers us a perfect example of what it means to be a spiritually mature, God-centered woman. Our Lady is not a woman who is full of *herself*; she's a woman who is full of *God's grace*. But her lack of self-focus does not make her a doormat. She's a woman of supernatural strength, dignity, and power.

Her power was on display in Luke 1:38 when she accepted God's invitation to be the mother of the Redeemer: "Behold, I am the handmaid of the Lord; let it be to me according to your word." Her power is in her surrender. Author and philosopher Carrie Gress explores this paradox:

> The world tells us that we are powerful when we are strong, full of vigor and life, and able to conquer or overcome those who are weaker than we are. Mary's strength is the inverse: "For when I am weak, then I am strong" (2 Cor. 12:10). Her strength is in her capacity to get her will out of the way and allow the will of her beloved Father to shine through her. The real power to bring order, love, and a true icon of God is found in the surrender.[40]

We'd be fools to surrender to someone who doesn't have our best interests at heart. If we question whether God's love is unconditional, if we aren't sure that He is truly *for* us, if we aren't sure if He is trustworthy, we're going to find it hard to emulate Mary. There are times in our lives when we struggle with doubt. When this is our experience, we need to continue to pray, turn to good spiritual mentors, keep receiving the sacraments, and remember the times God has shown up for us in the past. When we do these things regardless of whether we feel like it, we are keeping God as our first priority. Trust in Him is worth fighting for. The alternative is self-protecting and doing all we can to stay in control. Some might call this self-care, but it actually harms us on the soul level.

---

39 Josh Meyers, "Have We Made Authenticity an Idol?" *Relevant*, February 12, 2021, https://www.relevantmagazine.com/faith/have-we-made-authenticity-idol/.

40 Gress, *The Anti-Mary Exposed*, 126.

Mary was able to surrender because she loved God and wanted to do His will. She also knew beyond a doubt that she was loved by the Lord. And perhaps the transformation that we most need is "the power to comprehend with all the saints what is the breadth and length and height and depth, and to know the love of Christ which surpasses knowledge, that you may be filled with all the fulness of God" (Ephesians 3:18). This is my prayer for you, my friend.

## My Resolution

Examples:

1.  I commit to honoring the Sabbath. I want to set aside one day a week to obey God's command to rest and to experience the delight that comes through *being* instead of *doing*. To that end, I will think ahead on Saturday and prepare. I'll plan out what needs to be done for Monday morning, and I'll do it Saturday instead of Sunday. I'll make a list of things that delight me, and then look forward to doing them on the Sabbath.

2.  I find it difficult to see myself as God sees me. To help me start my day with a focus on what God says about my identity I will read Appendix 3: Who I Am in Christ.

3.  I want to treat my body as the temple of the Holy Spirit and to experience the fullness of His power working in my life. For an increase of the Holy Spirit, I'll daily pray these words by Saint Augustine:

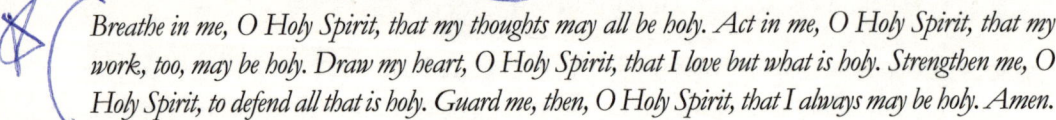

*Breathe in me, O Holy Spirit, that my thoughts may all be holy. Act in me, O Holy Spirit, that my work, too, may be holy. Draw my heart, O Holy Spirit, that I love but what is holy. Strengthen me, O Holy Spirit, to defend all that is holy. Guard me, then, O Holy Spirit, that I always may be holy. Amen.*

My Resolution:

# Catechism Clips

*CCC 1308* Although Confirmation is sometimes called the "sacrament of Christian maturity," we must not confuse adult faith with the adult age of natural growth, nor forget that the baptismal grace is a grace of free, unmerited election and does not need "ratification" to become effective. St. Thomas reminds us of this:

> Age of body does not determine age of soul. Even in childhood man can attain spiritual maturity: as the book of Wisdom says: "For old age is not honored for length of time, or measured by number of years." Many children, through the strength of the Holy Spirit they have received, have bravely fought for Christ even to the shedding of their blood.

*CCC 1487* The sinner wounds God's honor and love, his own human dignity as a man called to be a son of God, and the spiritual well-being of the Church, of which each Christian ought to be a living stone.

*CCC 1700* The dignity of the human person is rooted in his creation in the image and likeness of God (article 1); it is fulfilled in his vocation to divine beatitude (article 2). It is essential to a human being freely to direct himself to this fulfillment (article 3).

*CCC 2563* The heart is the dwelling-place where I am, where I live; according to the Semitic or Biblical expression, the heart is the place "to which I withdraw." The heart is our hidden center, beyond the grasp of our reason and of others; only the Spirit of God can fathom the human heart and know it fully. The heart is the place of decision, deeper than our psychic drives. It is the place of truth, where we choose life or death. It is the place of encounter, because as image of God we live in relation: it is the place of covenant.

 NOTES

# Lesson 4

# Priority 3: Your Marriage

## Introduction

Some years ago, my husband, Leo, and I volunteered with a marriage preparation program, offering coaching to a newly engaged couple. We started by asking them to share some examples of marriages that they admired. They sat in silence for some time, and finally admitted that they couldn't think of a single one. We found this sobering, and recent studies indicate that their experience is not unique. Marriage rates have been dropping, despite the fact that marriage has been proven to be economically beneficial, increases longevity, and results in a positive life outcome for children that is two to three times that of children from single-parent homes.[41] People are increasingly postponing marriage, and it is projected that many young adults will forgo marriage altogether.[42]

Some are pessimistic about marriage because of the bad ones they've seen up close. But for others it's because of unrealistic expectations of what a marriage should be. The search for the perfect soul mate can be never-ending, in large measure because the perfect person does not exist. When we think we've found "Mr. Right," we can inadvertently place expectations on him that no person will ever be able to live up to. Our relationships need to be properly ordered. If we aren't putting God first, we'll be tempted to look at a husband as a pseudo-savior. This puts pressure on a marriage to provide a level of fulfillment that is utterly unrealistic. The fact that 80 percent of

---

41  W. Bradford Wilcox, ed., *The State of Our Unions: Marriage in America 2009* (Charlottesville, VA: National Marriage Project; New York: Institute for American Values, 2009), http://www.stateofourunions.org/2009/SOOU2009.pdf.

42  Sally C. Curtin and Paul D. Sutton, "Marriage Rates in the United States, 1900–2018" (accessed March 10, 2021), https://www.cdc.gov/nchs/data/hestat/marriage_rate_2018/marriage_rate_2018.htm.

divorces are initiated by women indicates that something is very wrong with either our expectations or our experience of marriage.[43]

The way our culture defines the purpose of marriage has changed over time. In centuries past, the purpose of marriage was procreation and preservation. Marriages were often arranged, and were even used to secure political alliances across international borders. But much changed during the time of the Enlightenment (the seventeenth and eighteenth centuries), when the focus shifted to personal fulfillment and happiness. Self-actualization became the highest goal. As this pursuit became the norm, marriage primarily became "a personal contract between two equals seeking love, stability, and happiness."[44] If this is the definition of marriage, then when we don't feel love, stability, and happiness, it makes sense for the contract to be dissolved. But is this how God defines marriage?

If we want to experience what God intended for married couples, we have to take a look at what He says is the purpose of marriage. He is the one who instituted it—He created marriage—so we should pay careful attention to what He says it is for.[45] If we're off on this point, we'll find ourselves in a state of confusion, ill-equipped to navigate this complex relationship. But allowing our understanding of marriage to be molded by the maker of it changes everything in the most wonderful ways.

Leo and I have been married for almost thirty years. Has every day of it been rainbows and sunshine? No. We have navigated our fair share of disappointment and hurt. We both can speak from experience that those closest to us are the ones who can hurt us the most. But we have also tasted the glory that comes when you stick with it, learn from the challenges, and never give up. I am falling more and more in love with Leo every day—not with an "ideal soul mate," but with the glorious thing that God is doing in Leo's life. I see it more and more with each passing year. We've both changed and evolved; we're not the same people we were when we stood at the altar in our early twenties. And that's a good thing.

---

43 "Why Women File 80 Percent of Divorces," divorcesource.com, January 20, 2016, https://www.divorcesource.com/blog/why-women-file-80-percent-of-divorces/#:~:text=According%20to%20the%20National%20Center%20for%20Health%20Statistics%2C,percent%20of%20the%20divorces%20are%20initiated%20by%20women.

44 "How Marriage Has Changed over the Centuries," The Week, June 1, 2012, https://theweek.com/articles/475141/how-marriage-changed-over-centuries.

45 "God himself is the author of marriage…Marriage is not a purely human institution despite the many variations it may have undergone through the centuries in different cultures, social structures, and spiritual attitudes." (CCC 1603)

Because of God's grace, we don't need to finish as we've begun. There is always hope. God's arm is not too short to save.[46] This means that He can reach into your heart and into your husband's heart, and supernaturally connect the two. This is what He's in the business of doing. So, I pray you would not give up if you are currently discouraged. Let's invite Him to speak a fresh word to us by focusing on five critical questions that will shed light on what God has to say about marriage.

## Day One
## WHAT'S THE POINT OF MARRIAGE?

As we dive into the subject of marriage, we'll begin by exploring what God has to say about it. It might feel a little dry and laborious at first, but I ask you to stay with me. I know we want to get to the personal application (which is a good thing to want!), but we'll be better able to improve our marriages if we take some time to lay a solid foundation.

1.  A.  How is the first marriage described in Genesis 2:24?

    *A Man shall leave his mother + father and Cling to his wife. The 2 become one flesh.*

    B.  Do you observe any ways in which marriages today don't live up to that description?

2.  How is God described in CCC 221? What does it say we've been destined for?

    *God is described as an 'eternal exchange of love' between father, son + Holy Spirit — God has destined us to join in that exchange of love.*

    God is, by definition, relational. He invites us into the "eternal exchange of love" of the Trinity (CCC 221) and wants our marriages to reflect that love.

3.  A.  In God's eyes, marriage is much more than a contract. A contract involves an exchange of goods: you give me this, and I'll give you that. But as said earlier, God is all about relationships. He has always considered marriage a covenant rather than a contract. A covenant is an experience of relationship, not an exchange of goods. God asks that this relationship be characterized by

---

46  "No, the hand of the Lord is not too short to save." (Isaiah 59:1)

sacrificial love, and that can be tough to live out. How does Saint Paul describe this reality in Romans 7:15? *we often do the opposite of what we know we should do. we do what we want and do the things we hate (selfishness)*

B. God knew that what He asked of us in marriage was going to be difficult to accomplish. And so He elevated the covenant of marriage "to the dignity of a sacrament" (CCC 1601). You may wonder what difference that makes. It makes all the difference in the world. This is because a sacrament is a visible sign of an invisible reality that gains grace. It's a way that God infuses us with the ability to do something supernatural, something beyond our own ability. What grace do you need for your marriage right now? Think back to Saint Paul's words in Romans 7:15. What do you find yourself doing over and over even though you know it hurts your marriage? Ask God to infuse you with grace in this area of need.

The area where I repeatedly feel regret:

Dear God,
Please give me the grace to…

Another of the points of marriage is that we live it as a sacrament, not as a contract. Marriage is *not* a conditional commitment to stay together as long as your spouse keeps up with the things expected of him. In many ways, it's a promise made to God before it's a promise made to each other. This promise would be impossible to keep were it not for God's gift of grace, which allows us to persevere when we'd rather quit. Grace is given so that we can reflect Jesus to each other, even when the other seems least deserving.

4. What did Jesus teach about divorce in Mark 10:2–11? *Jesus said that what God has brought together, no man can seperate. Divorce + re-marrying is committing adultery.*

This passage requires some explanation. In the Old Testament, Moses (the one who delivered and communicated God's law to the Israelite people) made concessions for divorce. The people's hard hearts had brought them to a place where apparently divorce seemed the only option. But instead of upholding what Moses had said, Jesus quoted Genesis, which was going back to God's original design for marriage. Why did He feel it was possible to expect more of people when it had proven so hard in the past? Jesus knew He was soon going to make grace available to people—grace that the Old Testament Israelites hadn't had access to. The grace that was to be given in the sacrament of marriage was something new.

It's important to note that when the Church determines that a valid marriage never occurred, an annulment follows. There is no shame in this, and it can be an incredibly healing process. But in many ways, our civil laws of no-fault divorce have made it *too* easy to get out of a marriage. The topic of divorce should never be used as a threat. When divorce is threatened, everyone shuts down emotionally and starts to self-protect. We cannot self-protect and love at the same time, and so just when we most need to love heroically, we find ourselves unable to do so.

5.  A. Read the following quote from early twentieth-century Pope Pius XI, and record what he says is the chief reason for marriage:

> This mutual molding of husband and wife, this determined effort to perfect each other, can in a very real sense...be said to be the chief reason and purpose of matrimony, provided matrimony be looked at not in the restricted sense as instituted for the proper conception and education of the child, but more widely as the blending of life as a whole and the mutual interchange and sharing thereof.[47]

It's been said that nothing gives us more opportunity to grow in character than marriage. In so many other relationships, when someone speaks the truth to us about our own shortcomings, we have the option of walking away or distancing ourselves for a time. Not in marriage. One of the points of marriage is that we

---

47  Scott Hahn, *The First Society: The Sacrament of Matrimony and the Restoration of the Social Order* (Steubenville, OH: Emmaus, 2018), 47.

are helping each other to become more like Christ. This is a messy process, in which we need to learn to "speak the truth in love" (Ephesians 4:15) to each other.

B.  Have you ever had the experience of growing in character because of something you learned from your spouse? If so, share it here.

Were you able to thank your spouse for what he taught you? If it happened by means of a painful experience, that is probably hard to do. But if you can humble yourself and do so now, it could usher even more grace into your marriage.

*Quiet your heart and enjoy His presence…He never fails to supply the needed grace.*

*I recently had a conversation about marriage with Father John Riccardo, a wonderful priest, author, and evangelist. (He's the one who wrote* Rescued, *the book I reference in Lesson 2.) He shared that grace is given to a couple so they can make Jesus present to the other. The truth is, we all come to marriage with wounds and baggage. Father John's maternal grandparents were divorced, and that was during a time when it not only was painful for all involved but also carried a stigma. His dad knew how that experience had broken his mother's heart. Father John shared that his father knew, deep within, that God wanted to use him as a salve for her. He endeavored to love her in such a way that she could experience healing.*

*At his father's funeral, before the family was seated in the front of the church, they gathered at the back around the coffin. The coffin was open, and all the children watched their mother speak her final words to their father before it was closed. Seated in her wheelchair, she leaned over with words for her husband alone, although her children overheard. What were those final words?*

*"Honey, because of you, I know who God is."*

*This, in a nutshell, is the point of marriage—that we love in such a way that our spouse gets a glimpse of the unconditional love of God. Is this easy? No. We cannot do it in our own strength. But that's why marriage is a sacrament, not a contract. When God asks something of us, He provides what is needed. Nowhere is this truer than in marriage.*

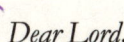

*Dear Lord,*
*"I can will what is right, but I cannot do it." (Romans 7:18)*
*I cannot do it alone. I cannot do it without You.*

*"But with God all things are possible" (Matthew 19:26). So I ask for an outpouring of Your grace into my marriage. [Tell Him of the specific area where you most need His healing touch.] Please infuse me with divine love so that I can reflect You in all my interactions with my husband, even when his faults seem worse than mine. Especially then, Lord. Amen.*

## Day Two
## WHAT IF I THINK I MARRIED THE WRONG PERSON?

The idea of finding your soul mate, marrying him, and living happily ever after has universal appeal. But is it possible? The odds are slim, according to a NASA scientist who calculated its likelihood. According to his research, if you lived ten thousand lifetimes, in one of those you'd find your soulmate.[48]

"We always marry the wrong person. We never know whom we marry; we just think we do."[49] This thought-provoking statement was made by Duke University ethics professor Stanley Hauerwas. The point he was making is that marriage is a tremendous change agent. In addition, we change over time, so the person you marry in his twenties or thirties is not going to be the same person in his fifties and sixties. He'll develop and evolve. And so will you. The goal? "Learning how to love and care for the stranger to whom you find yourself married."[50]

1. Do you agree with Stanley Hauerwas' observations? Why or why not?

2. We will all change throughout the course of our marriages. The question is, will we change for the better? Many a wife has seen the ways in which her husband should change, and then has set out to make it happen. This rarely works well

---

48  Maria Popova, "The Actual Algebra of Finding Your Soul Mate," BrainPickings (accessed March 11, 2021), https://www.brainpickings.org/2014/09/02/the-science-of-soul-mates-xkcd/.

49  Stanley Hauerwas, "Sex and Politics," *Christian Century*, April 19, 1978, 417–22, as cited by Tim Keller, *The Meaning of Marriage* (New York: Penguin Books, 2011), 32–3.

50  Hauerwas, "Sex and Politics."

because no one likes to be controlled. But our words do have tremendous power to *influence*. Read the following verses and note the ways in which your words can have power for the good.

Proverbs 12:18 *There is one whose rash words are like sword thrusts, but the tongue of the wise speaks/brings healing.*

What would be different in our marriages if instead of speaking rashly, we first prayed, asking God to help our words be wise and to bring healing?

Proverbs 15:1 *A soft answer turns away wrath, but a harsh word stirs up anger.*

Our tone and word choice matter. Being harsh often results in a spouse simply growing defensive or withdrawing. A gentle explanation with lower volume, slower speech, and less jacked-up emotion is often far more effective than an emotionally laden one.

Isaiah 50:4 *The Lord has given me a tongue of those who are taught that I may know how to sustain with a word him that is weary. Morning by morning he wakens my ear to hear as those who are taught.*

This verse implies that the speaker has taken the time to learn wisdom. She can then draw on that supply of truth to speak words that sustain others, helping the weary. "Morning by morning he wakens" is a picture of a woman getting up and first thing in the morning gaining God's perspective on her circumstances. She listens to His instruction before anything else.

Proverbs 29:11 *A fool gives full vent to his anger, but a wise man quietly holds it back.*

Does that verse mean that we just stuff our feelings? No…this next verse shows us the alternative.

Ephesians 4:15 *Rather, speaking the truth in love, we are to grow up in every way into him who is the head, into Christ.*

Some of us need to learn to speak more lovingly. Others need to speak more truthfully. It's up to us to commit to growing in whichever of the two areas is our weakness.

One lesson I have learned during almost three decades of marriage: I cannot control or change my husband. The only one I can change is myself. Paying attention to my words is a critical way that I do all I can to change for the better, day-by-day.

3. There comes a time in many marriages when one or both partners' eyes start to wander, wondering if there is someone better out there. We might fantasize about what it would be like to be married to someone else. My friends, this is very dangerous ground. Stop those destructive thoughts at the source. Reject them. Don't play around with them, because they lead you right into the enemy's lair.

When we are focused on our spouse's shortcomings and are comparing him to men who seem far more compatible with us, we are failing to see those men's shortcomings. Pastor Tim Keller has wise words to share on this subject:

> But the great thing about the model of Christian marriage…is that when you envision the "someone better," you can think of the future version of the person to which you are already married. The someone better is the spouse you already have. God has indeed given us a desire for the perfect spouse, but you should seek it in the one to whom you're married. Why discard this partner for someone else only to discover that person's deep, hidden flaws? Some people with serial marriages go through the cycle of infatuation, disillusionment, rejection, and flight to someone else—over and over. The only way you're going to actually begin to see another person's glory-self is to stick with him or her.[51]

A. Reflect on the positive changes you have seen in your spouse throughout the course of your marriage. Record them here.

B. Consider taking the time to write a letter to your husband, telling him about how these changes cause you to fall in love with him all over again. Tell him

---

51  Timothy Keller, *The Meaning of Marriage* (New York: Penguin Books, 2011), 159.

that you are excited as you think about your future, knowing that there are going to be new things that you discover about him. Thank him for tapping into the strength and humility it takes to grow. Share with him how this helps your respect for him to deepen. Your words matter. They have the power to build up or destroy.

Write out Proverbs 18:21 here.

*Death and life are in the power of The tongue, and those who love it will eat its fruits.*

What will be your choice? Words of life or words of death?

4. What command is given by Jesus in Mark 12:31?

*Love your neighbor as yourself.*

Since there is no one dwelling in closer proximity to you than your spouse, it is fair to say that he is considered your "neighbor." So, what do you do when you feel like the one who really needs some love and TLC is you, and you don't feel like offering it to your husband?

An important principle to remember is that feelings follow actions. We will always be tempted to wait to do the "loving thing" until we are *feeling* loving. But this is a bad plan, because you could be in for a good long wait. But incredibly, something rather miraculous happens when we just *do* the loving thing. Our feelings start to follow. Why? Because obedience to God softens our hearts. In the words of C. S. Lewis,

> Though natural likings should normally be encouraged, it would be quite wrong to think that the way to become charitable is to sit trying to manufacture affection feelings…The rule for all of us is perfectly simple. Do not waste time bothering whether you "love" your neighbor; act as if you did. As soon as we do this we find one of the great secrets. When you are behaving as if you loved someone, you will presently come to love him.[52]

What are some actions you could take to actively love your husband today?

Here are some ideas to get you started:

---

52  C. S. Lewis, *Mere Christianity* (San Francisco: HarperCollins, 2001), 130–1.

- Give him a backrub.
- Write him a letter of affirmation and mail it to him at work.
- Give the gift of listening, asking about his highs and lows of the day, without adding any corrective comments.
- Buy him his favorite snack and serve it to him in the evening.
- Ask him what practical thing you could do to serve him—something he doesn't like to do for himself.

To actively show my husband love, I will:

*Quiet your heart and enjoy His presence…Invite Him to change the way you see your husband.*

*"So we do not lose heart. Though our outer man is wasting away, our inner man is being renewed every day. For this slight momentary affliction is preparing for us an eternal weight of glory beyond all comparison." (2 Corinthians 4:16–17)*

*If you have been married awhile, you are likely seeing changes in your spouse's appearance (not to mention your own). When our kids look at our old wedding photos, they are quick to point out that my hair was brown (!) and their dad looked around twelve. They look at us now and see wrinkles and softer middles and the occasional gray hair. I can see these things as well, but I don't really notice them because it's far more interesting to see the ways Leo and I are growing more like Jesus. Tim Keller describes my experience better than I can: "Spiritually discerning spouses can see a bit of what God sees in their partners, and it excites them. The rest of the world sees us wrinkling up, but using marriage's powers in the grace of Jesus, we see each other become more and more spiritually gorgeous…What we should say to each other on our wedding day is, 'As great as you look today, someday you will stand with me before God in such beauty that it will make these clothes look like rags.'"[53]*

*Dear Lord,*
*This is the perspective that I want to have when I look at my husband. Help my eyes to be renewed so that I'm not focusing on his weaknesses but instead am looking for (and acknowledging) the areas where he has grown. Help me to look back and see how far he has come. Fill me with hope that with You, things can change. I claim the promise of Philippians 1:6 that "He who began a good work in [my husband] will bring it to completion at the day of Jesus Christ." Keep my eyes on eternity and on the power of Your grace. Amen.*

---

53  Keller, *The Meaning of Marriage*, 189.

# Day Three
## IS IT ALWAYS GOING TO BE THIS HARD?

Our capacity to endure suffering in marriage increases if we know when the tough season will end. It saps us of hope when we feel like it will last forever. Feelings of hopelessness can cause women to seek escape through fantasizing about another partner, having an emotional or physical affair, or contemplating divorce. In his book *Interior Freedom*, Father Jacques Philippe writes, "As long as hope remains, love develops. If hope is extinguished, love grows cold. A world without hope soon becomes a world without love."[54] Apply this truth to marriage and you see how critical it is that we are able to anticipate things getting better. Here on earth, we need hope in order to love well.

In this portion of the lesson, we're going to explore why we can have hope for our marriages. We're going to examine this from a biblical perspective, but I also want to point out that longitudinal studies have found that two out of three unhappily married couples who avoided divorce or separation ended up happily married five years later.[55] Interestingly, "other research (and the experience of clinicians) suggests that the kinds of marital troubles that lead to divorce cannot be sharply distinguished from the marital troubles that spouses overcome."[56] This means that whatever you face, it is possible that your marriage can not only survive, but experience significant restoration. Nothing is beyond the reach of God's mercy.

1. A. Where should our confidence come from? See Job 11:18.

   *We can have confidence because there is hope. We will be protected & can Rest on safety.*

   B. Where should our hope come from? See Psalm 71:5.

   *God is our hope. Christ Jesus is our hope.*

2. A. According to 1 Peter 1:3, we are "born anew" to what?

   *To a living hope.*

---

54  Father Jacques Philippe, *Interior Freedom* (New York: Scepter, 2002), 107.

55  Linda J. Waite et al., *Does Divorce Make People Happy? Findings from a Study of Unhappy Marriages* (New York: Institute for American Values, 2002), http://americanvalues.org/catalog/pdfs/does_divorce_make_people_happy.pdf.

56  Waite et al., *Does Divorce Make People Happy?*

B. Being born anew to a living hope is made possible because of which monumental moment in history? See the second part of 1 Peter 1:3.

*Because of the resurrection of Jesus*

What's more final and definitive than death? What seems less possible to change or reverse than death? No matter what we face or what we imagine might be around the corner, it is not too much for Jesus, because death was not too much for Him. This is why His resurrection should give us hope. In the words of Father Jacques Philippe, "Ultimately, we can really forgive people only because Christ rose from the dead; his Resurrection is the guarantee that God can cure every wrong and every hurt."[57]

3. The rebirth of a marriage can happen supernaturally through the work of the Holy Spirit. Christian rebirth is "a rebirth to love."[58] Because the Holy Spirit is within us, we can be cleansed of bitterness and unforgiveness. We are given a supernatural ability to sacrifice for one another, because of God's love within us.

This opportunity to begin life anew is not a onetime offer. We can always hit the do-over button with Jesus. As is promised in Lamentations 3:22–24, "The steadfast love of the lord never ceases, his mercies never come to an end; they are new every morning; great is [His] faithfulness." In what way does your marriage need a fresh start?

4. A. According to Matthew 7:24–25, what does a wise man build his house on?

*Wise man builds his house on the Rock.*

B. How does Jesus describe a woman who builds her life on the rock?

*She hears Jesus' words and puts them into practice.*

C. The storms will come regardless of where we build. What storms are you facing in your marriage right now? Where are you in need of hope?

---

57 Philippe, *Interior Freedom*, 65.

58 William Barclay, *The New Daily Study Bible: The Letters of James and Peter* (Louisville, KY: Westminster John Knox Press, 2017), 198, 200.

*Quiet your heart and enjoy His presence…He's a shelter in the storm.*

The conversation I had with Father John Riccardo continued with a discussion about the inevitability of storms descending on our marriages, no matter where we build. He shared that his parents almost divorced a year after getting married. But instead of giving up, they chose to lean in and learn through the difficulties. What they learned was that it was possible to trust God, and because of that, to trust each other. They weathered the storm, and as a result, things got better.

Many decades later, when going through his parents' things, he found an anniversary card written by his father after sixty-six years of marriage. His dad wrote, "How is it possible that after 66 years of marriage I can love you now more than ever?"

Father John assured me, "We can always anticipate things getting better. Not easier, but better."

This makes me think of wise words from my counselor, spoken to me when I was in the midst of a storm in my own marriage. I was sharing with her how hard I felt it was. She said something that has given me great food for thought: "Why do we equate hard with bad? What if hard is actually good? What if hard is what brings the good that we most desire?"

It might be that things are always going to be hard. I can't promise you that the trials will lift. But I can assure you, if you are willing to learn from each and every storm, you will come out stronger and better. The reward will be the woman you are becoming, and the gift of continuing in a marriage that more often than not becomes sweeter with time. Father Jacques Philippe wisely writes, "The most painful suffering is the suffering we reject."[59] But when we accept it as a gift (albeit with packaging we dislike), we can receive the lessons and growth it contains. This makes all the difference.

Dear Lord,

I ask for Your grace to help me fight against the discouragement and worries that rob me of hope and sap my energy. Help me instead to remember that the grace You provide is sufficient for the day. You give me grace bit by bit and ask that I keep coming to You for more. This is the daily discipline of depending on You.

Help me to trust that in the end, things will work out all right, because You are the One in control. You conquered death, and my problems are not too much for You. Please fill me with the peace that surpasses understanding, so that I can reflect that peace to others. Amen.

---

59   Philippe, *Interior Freedom*, 46.

# Day Four
## WHAT'S THE MOST IMPORTANT INGREDIENT FOR A SUCCESSFUL MARRIAGE?

*"Let us remember that love lives through sacrifice and is nourished by giving…Without sacrifice there is no love."* —*Saint Maximilian Kolbe*

The priest who married Leo and me summarized all his marriage prep for us with the following instructions: "If you, Leo, make it your life mission to do what is best for Lisa, and you, Lisa, focus on doing what is best for Leo, your marriage should go well." In the courtship and infatuation stages of our relationship, this seemed like an easy thing to accomplish. But as time went on, our desire to get our own way surfaced pretty quickly. Doing what was best for the other often required setting our own wants and needs aside. And we discovered something about each other: we are both profoundly self-centered. As I reflect on the problems we've faced over the years of our marriage, at the root of it was often a refusal to serve and a focus on self.

We've found that an essential ingredient for a successful marriage is self-sacrifice. But before we dive in to hear God's perspective on this subject, I would be remiss if I did not note that these principles do not apply to relationships when abuse is present. I pray and trust that these verses will not be taken out of context to justify harmful and destructive patterns of behavior.

1. What instructions are given in Romans 12:1–2? What perspective do these verses give regarding how countercultural it is to live sacrificially? What's the reward for living this way? *We are told to offer our bodies as a living sacrifice, as a form of worship; not to be conformed by this world but to be transformed by the renewal of our minds*

2. Read Philippians 2:3–8 and answer the following questions.

    A. What should never be our motive in our dealings with other people? What virtue are we encouraged to have, and how is that virtue lived out? See Philippians 2:3. *We should never be motivated by selfishness or deceit, we should display the virtue of humility*

B. Philippians 2:4 says that we should not look just at our own interests, but also to the interests of others. In your marriage, over which issue do you most often see this tug-of-war take place?

C. Who is to be our example in this radical way of living, and how specifically was it lived out? Is more asked of us than was asked of Him? See Philippians 2:5–8.

*Jesus, — our servant God. He humbled himself to obedience & died on the cross for us*

3. Write out the following verses that speak of self-sacrificial love, and share a specific way you could live out that instruction in your marriage this week.

Matthew 16:24 *If any man come after me, let him deny himself, take up his cross & follow me*

Ephesians 5:1–2 *Therefore be imitators of God, as beloved children, Walk in love, as Christ loved us and gave himself up for us, a fragrant offering and sacrifice to God.*

4. There are little compromises you'll make in marriage that are inconvenient but don't really qualify as suffering. Other times, laying down your own rights will be deeply painful. Often the difficulty is magnified by the fact that it seems as if it's always *you* who gives in. You might be wondering if it's worth it. At these times, I have found the Church's teaching on redemptive suffering to be very helpful. Perhaps when you were growing up you were told to "offer it up" whenever anything went wrong. We're going to explore what that means.

A. The foundation for this teaching can be found in Colossians 1:24. Write the verse out here. *Now, I rejoice in my sufferings for your sake, and in my flesh I complete what is lacking in Christ's afflictions for the sake of his body, the church.*

This verse is easy to misunderstand, and as a result is often skipped over and ignored. But if we dig in and seek to grasp its meaning, we just might find a nugget of truth that can be truly transformative for our marriages.

B. To start with, we need to state what this verse does not say. It does *not* mean that what Jesus did on the cross was not sufficient for our salvation. Read the following excerpt from Saint John Paul's encyclical on redemptive suffering (*Salvifici Doloris*) and underline the sentences that make that point clear:

> The sufferings of Christ created the good of the world's redemption. This good is in itself inexhaustible and infinite. No man can add anything to it. But at the same time, in the mystery of the Church as His body, Christ has in a sense opened his own redemptive suffering to all human suffering...
>
> Does this mean that the redemption achieved by Christ is not complete? No. It only means that the redemption accomplished through satisfactory love, remains always open to all love expressed in human suffering. [60]

When Jesus suffered on Calvary, He obtained the graces that allow us to be forgiven and saved. *We* did not obtain those graces, *He* did. We do not earn our salvation; Jesus gives it to us as a gift. But He invites us to unite our sufferings to His own in order to release those graces in a powerful way. When we are willing to suffer patiently and offer it to Christ, things happen in the spiritual realm. Graces are released. This means that our suffering can have tremendous meaning and impact.

C. In the words of Dr. Mark Miravalle, "Practically speaking, your sufferings could be applied to someone on the other side of the world who is dying and who needs some particular grace to say yes to God at that moment his life."[61] But it doesn't have to be applied to someone on the other side of the world, as beautiful as that is. You can ask Jesus to apply that grace to your own marriage. That's the value of your suffering.

What current suffering could you choose to endure patiently, offering it up, in order for supernatural grace to be released? Where would you like to see that grace applied?

---

60 John Paul II, *Salvifici Doloris* (Encyclical Letter on the Christian Meaning of Human Suffering), sec. 24, February 11, 1984, http://www.vatican.va/content/john-paul-ii/en/apost_letters/1984/documents/hf_jp-ii_apl_11021984_salvifici-doloris.html.

61 Mark Miravalle, "Coredeemers in Christ" (lecture, Franciscan University of Steubenville, Steubenville, OH).

*Quiet your heart and enjoy His presence…He invites you to participate in the transformation of your marriage.*

*Dr. Bob Schuchts' teaching on redemptive suffering has been life-changing for me. He teaches that suffering is always evil, and God is not the source of evil. God may allow it, but He is not its author. Redemptive suffering is not a glorification of suffering—it's a glorification through suffering. But we have a choice in how we will respond to it. We can respond in the way that Satan wants us to: "I was wounded, so now I'll wound." Or we can respond the way God desires, by participating in redemption. In the words of Dr. Bob, "We are either a part of redemption or a part of evil."[62]*

*So often, we sin because we are trying to escape suffering. Building on what we learned from Father Jacques Philippe in Day Three:*

> *What really hurts is not so much suffering itself as the fear of suffering. If welcomed trustingly and peacefully, suffering makes us grow. It matures and trains us, purifies us, teaches us how to love unselfishly, makes us poor in heart, humble, gentle, and compassionate toward our neighbor. Fear of suffering, on the other hand, hardens us in self-protective, defensive attitudes, and often leads us to make irrational choices with disastrous consequences.[63]*

*Dear Lord,*
*I long to love sacrificially and put the needs of my husband ahead of my own. I find this incredibly hard to do. In fact, it is impossible without Your help. So I ask for Your strength to suffer well—to offer up my hardships and endure them with patience. I ask that the graces from that sacrifice be released into my marriage so that more and more, we display the kind of love that will cause those around us to see You in our midst. Amen.*

# Day Five
# WHAT DIFFERENCE DOES FORGIVENESS MAKE?

*"Everyone says that forgiveness is a lovely idea, until they have something to forgive."* —*C. S. Lewis*

1. What do the following verses teach us about forgiveness?

   Matthew 6:14–15

---

62  Bob Schuchts, "Redemptive Suffering and Healing" (lecture, Good Shepherd Catholic Church, Tallahassee, FL, March 15, 2017).

63  Philippe, *Interior Freedom*, 47.

Matthew 18:21–22

2. What do we learn from Romans 12:19 in terms of our desire to make people pay for what they have done to us?

When we forgive, we are not saying that what happened didn't matter. We are not condoning the actions. What we are doing is relinquishing the right to be the one to hand out the punishment. We are allowing God to be the judge, instead of us. We leave the punishment to Him, instead of doing the punishing ourselves through things like the silent treatment, withholding physical affection, passive aggression, sneers, and insults.

3. What do the following verses say will happen if we refuse to forgive?

Sirach 28:2–3

Matthew 18:23–34

Ephesians 4:26–27

4. Forgiveness in marriage is like oil for a car engine. It's absolutely critical if we want things to run well. Positive feelings may or may not accompany forgiveness. Because forgiveness is a decision, not an emotion, it remains valid either way. Yet Dr. Sue Johnson points out this important truth:

> Certain incidents do more than just touch our raw spots or "hurt our feelings." They injure us so deeply that they overturn our world. They are relationship traumas. In the dictionary a trauma is defined as a wound that plunges us into fear and helplessness, that challenges all our assumptions of predictability and control…Every day hurts are easily dismissed and raw spots can fade away…but unresolved traumas do not heal…

> Sometimes partners do succeed in compartmentalizing traumas, but this results in a cool and distant relationship. And the barricade works only for a while. Injured feelings break out at some point when attachment needs come to the fore.[64]

This means that while forgiveness must readily be offered, there are times when the work of healing must also occur. Forgiveness is a part of this journey, but something more than words and a decision is required.

Dr. Johnson outlines six steps in the forgiveness process,[65] and although I will share them briefly here, if this is an area where you feel blocked, I highly recommend that you read her book *Created for Connection: The "Hold Me Tight" Guide for Christian Couples*.

Step 1: The injured partner is to speak his or her pain as openly and simply as possible. This means discussing what was felt and experienced, rather than building a case against your spouse and listing all that he or she did wrong.

Step 2: "The injuring partner stays emotionally present and acknowledges the wounded partner's pain and his or her part in it."[66]

Step 3: The injured partner acknowledges that in the moment of trauma, he or she made a vow to never feel like this again. He or she makes every effort to identify specifically which vow was made ("I will never…"). The vow might have to do with trust, or relying on the other, or being open about emotions. Whatever vow was made, a commitment is made to break that vow, reversing its harmful effects.

Step 4: The injuring partner takes ownership of what happened, and expresses regret and remorse.

Step 5: The injured partner tells his or her spouse what it is that he or she needs in order to bring closure to the trauma. This might be a need to hear something specifically said, or a need to be held.

Step 6: The couple commits to writing a new story. This new story allows the current interaction to take the place of the old story. It's letting the old narrative go so that a new one can take its place.

---

64  Johnson and Sanderfer, *Created for Connection*, 183, 185.

65  Johnson and Sanderfer, *Created for Connection*, 189–94.

66  Johnson and Sanderfer, *Created for Connection*, 190.

As you reflect on these steps, do you find that you have skipped over some of them and are experiencing a coolness and a distance in your marriage as a result? If so, which one(s)?

*Quiet your heart and enjoy His presence…Forgive others as the Lord has forgiven you.*

*"Forgiveness is the restoration of freedom to oneself. It is the key held in our own hand to our prison cell." —Saint John Paul II*

*I believe that many of us are locked in the prison cell of an old narrative. There's a story we keep going back to, a time when we desperately needed our loved one to give us support and he failed to do so. If we were to retell the story, it might sound to some as if we were overreacting. But the feeling of abandonment occurred, and its consequences can be felt for decades. This can cause us to remain stuck in patterns of behavior that we think are keeping us safe, but they are actually keeping us isolated. I speak of this from experience. I know what those prison walls look like.*

*The day I realized I was holding the key to my cell door, I felt terrified. With knowledge comes responsibility, and I knew I had a choice to make. I could take the risk of having the vulnerable dialogue described by Dr. Sue Johnson, or I could stay in my prison cell. I chose to speak.*

*Oh, my friend. I know how scary it is to be vulnerable in this way. I know the risk of coming out of hiding and asking to be seen. But I also know that the risk is worth it. In the words of author Gary Thomas, "Christian marriage is…about learning to fall forward. Obstacles arise, anger flares up, and weariness dulls our feelings and our senses. When this happens the spiritually immature respond by pulling back, becoming more distant from their spouse…Yet maturity is reached by continuing to move forward past the pain and apathy. Falls are inevitable. We can't control that, but we can control the direction in which we fall—toward or away from our spouse."*[67]

*I know it feels like a free fall. I know you wonder what happens on the other side of vulnerability. I can't predict how your words will be received, but one thing I know for certain: God will be there. His arms will catch you. Each and every time.*

*Lord, just give us a little more courage than fear.*

---

67  Gary Thomas, *Sacred Marriage* (Grand Rapids, MI: Zondervan, 2000), 155.

# Conclusion

*"The God of all grace who called you to his eternal glory through Christ [Jesus] will himself restore, confirm, strengthen, and establish you after you have suffered a little." (1 Peter 5:10)*

The goodness on the other side is worth the work to get there. I have asked myself the five questions we explored in this lesson, and I've wrestled with the answers. There was a time when I debated just settling for status quo. It seemed like a lot of the marriages around me had done that. They weren't thriving, but they were surviving. And that was something, right?

I am so glad I didn't settle.

Today I can honestly say that Leo is my best friend and my safe place. We have seen each other at our weakest and least attractive and we have done the work of *staying*. We have allowed the other to be human, and we've become a soft place to land for each other. Our kids roll their eyes at us because the affection and enjoyment of each other gets to be a little too much at times and is just so embarrassing to them. But deep down, they love it, and I know it makes them feel secure. It's the gift they need most from Leo and me—the knowledge that they can count on our love. They can trust that we are going to stay steady at the wheel.

God has confirmed, strengthened, and established us. But He didn't do it without our cooperation. And sometimes that cooperation felt a lot like suffering. But like 1 Peter 5:10 says, it's only for a little while. It won't last forever. And if we will press on, if we will fall forward, if we will doggedly not give up, there can be glory on the other side.

If you're still waiting for the glory to show up, then I encourage you to live out 1 Peter 5:6–7, to "humble yourselves under the mighty hand of God, that in due time he may exalt you. Cast all your anxieties on him, for he cares about you." He sees it all, He carries your heart, and He is at work. Right here, right now.

# My Resolution

Examples:

1.  I want my words to speak life, not death, to my husband. I commit to pausing before I speak in order to check if my words are going to build him up or tear him down. This does not mean I only say positive things, but it does mean that truth must be spoken in love.

2.  I want the power of redemptive suffering to be unleashed in my marriage. Because of this, I will offer up my self-sacrifices willingly and patiently, asking that this mysteriously release grace back into my marriage.

3.  I have discovered an area of my heart that needs to forgive and be healed. I commit to going through the six steps outlined by Dr. Sue Johnson in *Created for Connection: The "Hold Me Tight" Guide for Christian Couples.*

My Resolution:

# Catechism Clips

*CCC 221* God has revealed his innermost secret: God himself is an eternal exchange of love, Father, Son and Holy Spirit, and he has destined us to share in that exchange.

*CCC 1601* "The matrimonial covenant, by which a man and a woman establish between themselves a partnership of the whole of life, is by its nature ordered toward the good of the spouses and the procreation and education of offspring; this covenant between baptized persons has been raised by Christ the Lord to the dignity of a sacrament."

*CCC 2367* Called to give life, spouses share in the creative power and fatherhood of God. "Married couples should regard it as their proper mission to transmit human life and to educate their children; they should realize that they are thereby cooperating with the love of God the Creator and are, in a certain sense, its interpreters. They will fulfill this duty with a sense of human and Christian responsibility."

The thief only comes to STEAL & KILL AND DESTROY; I came that they MAY HAVE LIFE, AND have it Abundantly

JOHN 10:10

# Lesson 5

## PRIORITY 4: YOUR CHILDREN

### Introduction

*Here's to good women*
*May we know them*
*May we be them*
*May we raise them*

This popular quote hangs in my office, reminding me of the importance of what I model for my daughters. My example is equally important for my sons. These words have led me to reflect on what my kids see when they look at me. Do they see a woman filled with peace? Do they realize how much I *enjoy* being their mother and spending time with them? Do they know that the sacrifices I make for them, I make without resentment and with my whole heart? My desire is that my kids would see me as a strong and selfless woman who is able to navigate the obstacles of life with grace and dignity. I want them to know that any good they see in me comes from Jesus, because He is real and at the center of my life. I don't just want them to see good; I want them to see joy.

Why does this matter? Because the world is telling my kids a different story. This narrative says that fulfillment is found through accomplishments more than relationships. Mothers are encouraged to put themselves first, and some question when *mother* became synonymous with *martyr*. It's a move away from the family, which could very well cause our children to follow suit, preferring a "chosen family" of friends over a disjointed home life.

When I first started having children in the early nineties, I often went to the Christian bookstore to find some inspiration on how to be a good Christian mother. There was always a shelf devoted to this. Those books shaped my parenting philosophy. But when I go to the bookstore today, the books are hard to find. Contemporary Christian authors are more likely to write about the pursuit of dreams, discovering our gifts, and self-care. Please hear me. I am not saying that these topics don't matter. But I am saying that there has been a shift in our culture away from valuing selflessness, replacing it with self-focus.

I grow concerned when service to one's family is described as martyrdom. The message being fed to women is that giving ourselves fully and repeatedly to our children sets a bad example for them—that we should be getting what we want and asking for more.

But who is tending to the hearts at home?

If we do not, we will lose this next generation to whatever the current culture says matters most. If we aren't going to prioritize shaping our children's minds and hearts, the culture will step in and do it for us. Indeed, it already is happening, through the smartphones that are essentially extra appendages for most of our kids. I am deeply concerned for what is already being called "the lost generation." This is going down on our watch. But it is in our power to change the direction of the current in our own homes.

If we just go with the flow, we'll spend the majority of our time driving kids to various practices and watching them as they perform and compete. Whatever the activity, whether sports or the arts, the time commitment required will likely preclude family dinners and the downtime that allows for deeper conversation. More often than not, the problem is not that mothers don't care about tending to children's hearts. It's that we're too busy to do anything about it, and we don't know how to get out of schedules that often feel forced upon us.

But we *do* have a choice. We get to decide what matters most. Our children are on loan to us from God. This means that they don't "belong" to us, they aren't a way for us to prove our worth, and we are not to live vicariously through them. Our job is to lead them to Christ. Doing this is no easy task. It takes time and sacrifice. This can't be bought with cash; it requires time.

Because leading children to God isn't what the world around us values, it will almost always mean going against the tide. The right choices will often feel like weird countercultural ones. We should expect to be in the minority. But I believe making the choice to slow down and lean in at home holds the key to the joy we so desire.

But even as I write out that vision, I am aware that it can feel like just one more weight is being placed on shoulders that are already drooping. So here's the thing. Something has to roll off our backs before we can grasp hold of a new way to live. I am voting for kicking some expectations to the curb. The truth is, more than needing to play on the elite sports team, or getting into the top college, or owning the latest gaming system, or grabbing hold of every possible opportunity, or keeping up with the Joneses, or having every desire satisfied, your child needs *you*. Plain old normal you, grabbing hold of opportunities to point him or her to the things that really matter. This we can do, if we'll let the lesser things go.

Note: If you don't have kids under your roof, I encourage you to look for opportunities to pour into the children God has allowed to cross your path. This might be godchildren, grandchildren, or kids in your neighborhood or community. If you look around, I think you'll find that there are many kids who desperately need to be championed and mentored. Sometimes the timeliest influence isn't a parent. Ask God to reveal to you which children need what your hands and heart can offer.

## Day One
## LEADING YOUR CHILD TO GOD IN THE EARLY YEARS (0–5)

These are formative years, when kids are utterly dependent on the adults in their lives. During this time, it's important that they learn that God is trustworthy and good. The way they learn this is by seeing these traits in their parents. Children learn that God is kind and dependable when their parents model these attributes.

1.  A.  God is our Father, and we learn to love by following His example. Read Deuteronomy 32:10–11, which is a description of God caring for His children. Record the phrases that describe His tenderness, protectiveness, and attentiveness.

    *When God found His children in the wilderness, He encircled them & cared for them. He kept them as the apple of His eye. When we fall, He catches us and carries us on eagles wings*

    B.  What are some practical ways this type of care could be shown to a small child?

    *We can comfort & Hold them when they are afraid. We can delight in them — Lighting up & smiling when we see them*

2.  A.  God is described as a parent in Hosea 11:3–4. What images are used to describe Him? (Note: Ephraim is one of the twelve tribes of Israel. These tribes make up the nation of the Israelites—God's chosen people, His children).

    *God teaching his children to walk, picking them up when they fall. God leads with compassion*

B. What are some practical ways this type of care could be shown to a young child?

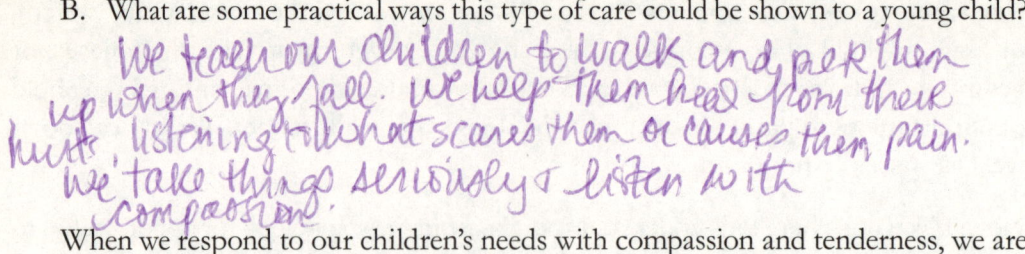

*We teach our children to walk and pick them up when they fall. We keep them heal from their hurts, listening to what scares them or causes them pain. We take things seriously + listen with compassion.*

When we respond to our children's needs with compassion and tenderness, we are leading them to God. They are learning that we are trustworthy, and we pray that one day they will transfer that trust to God. The time we spend pouring into small children, listening to them, cuddling them, smiling at them, taking them seriously, and enjoying them are all spiritual endeavors. These acts of kindness have eternal consequences.

3. Children need unconditional love, and they also need to be kept out of danger. Sometimes this means stepping in and protecting our kids, but it also requires that we discipline them, so they learn to make choices that keep them safe. Again, God is our example in this.

A. What do you learn about discipline from Proverbs 3:11–12?

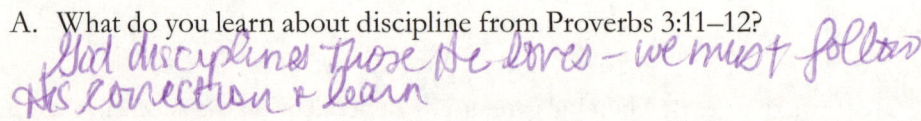

*God disciplines those He loves – we must follow His correction + learn*

B. What is the purpose of God's discipline of His children? See Hebrews 12:10–11.

*God disciplines us for good, so that we may become holy. We are being trained in righteousness.*

C. Hebrews 12:11 says that "for the moment, all discipline seems painful rather than pleasant." Do you feel guilty causing pain and discomfort to your child when you discipline? What do you think is the stronger motivator of your behavior—a desire that your child be happy, or that your child learn to obey?

God's discipline of us springs from love, and this must be true of our own. We say no, administer consequences, and do so consistently (otherwise we confuse our kids), and we do all these things out of love. We teach our kids what the standards are and why they exist (for their safety and growth), and what the consequences will be if those standards are broken. Both positive reinforcement for good choices and unpleasant consequences for bad ones are needed.

A note for the weary: If you are doing this well, you will likely feel you are constantly disciplining. I encourage you to hang in there. You aren't just disciplining, you are discipling, which is the process of helping someone learn to follow Jesus. Discipline will be painful for all involved in the short term, but if we stick with it, we all will be happier in the long run.

4.  Matthew 5:37 says, "Let your 'Yes' mean 'Yes,' and your 'No' mean 'No.' Anything more is from the evil one." This instruction has great application for parenting. When kids know the rules and the consequences and this stays consistent, it gives a sense of security. Can you identify any area of your parenting where you have been inconsistent with your discipline?

It's also important to note that these are years when children are sponges. Their brains are soaking up huge amounts of information, and it's being absorbed continuously and without effort. This is your best time to pour in, without receiving a critique back (those of you with older kids know what I'm talking about). Be sure to check out Appendix 4 for some great resources to help you talk to your kids about God. I've used every one of them with my children at one time or another, so they are tried and true.

*Quiet your heart and enjoy His presence…He is your loving Father.*

*"For you did not receive a spirit of slavery to fall back into fear, but you received a spirit of adoption, through which we cry, 'Abba! Father!'" (Romans 8:15)*

*This verse encourages us to approach God as our father. It is as we receive love from Him that we are able to share that love with our children.*

*Dear Lord,*
*I want to love my children the way You love me. You care for me tenderly and are concerned with all the details of my life. But You love me too much to leave me to my own devices. When You can see that my choices are hurting me, You discipline me to draw me back to the better path. Help me to learn the lessons You are trying to teach me. May I receive them as evidence of Your love.*

*I am weary, Lord, so I am crawling into Your lap. I feel like what is expected of me is beyond my own abilities. So I lay my head down on Your chest, and ask You to take care of everything. Give me the strength I need to love and discipline consistently. And when I fail (which I will certainly do) help me to turn to You for mercy, instead of beating myself up. May I rest in and receive Your delight. Amen.*

# Day Two
# THE ELEMENTARY SCHOOL YEARS (5–12)

The elementary school years are rife with opportunity for your child's spiritual development. You are still the primary influence in your child's life, which means this is a perfect window of time to teach him or her all you can. The next season is one in which your child will begin to question everything as he or she begins to think more critically.

Although you may feel awkward talking about God or feel underqualified to explain spiritual things, I want to encourage you to do it anyway. The truth is, you might feel self-conscious, but your child isn't assessing you. He or she is simply listening. You don't have to be perfect or even terribly knowledgeable. Just commit to passing on what you do know. You might be surprised how much that is!

**Read Deuteronomy 6:4–12.**

1.  A.  Reflecting on Deuteronomy 6:4–6, what is the starting point for teaching your children about God?

    *God's words are to be imprinted first in our own hearts.*

    B.  What habits have you established to make sure that you are daily allowing God's Word to be impressed on your own heart?

    *Prayer, reflection, listening to Halo. Call into a saint for guidance in everything.*

Author Jen Pollock Michel writes about how hard it is to *think* or *feel* your way into faith. This is both because we often don't know where to begin and because thoughts and feelings can be hard to control. She said the better course of action is to *practice* your way into faith because our habits can lead us to God.[68] I was discussing this with my youngest daughter, who asked me if I read the Bible every day. When I told her that I do, she said, "Well, I could never do that, because I have activities after school, and I don't have time." I assured her that if I waited until the afternoon, I would never have time either. But first thing in the morning, I can *make* time. She then said that she didn't have time in the morning, either. When I pointed out that she often did have a couple

---

68  Jen Pollock Michel, *A Habit Called Faith* (Grand Rapids, MI: Baker Books, 2021), 151.

of minutes that she spent reading a book by the fire, she realized that she could choose which book she picked up—the Bible or The Adventures of Captain Underpants.

2. Deuteronomy 6:7 says, "you shall teach them diligently to your children." What truths are we to diligently teach?

*we are to teach that God is one Lord and that we are to love Him with all our hearts, mind, body + soul.*

A critical truth to teach our children is that what God wants most from us is our love. He wants to have a relationship with us. One way we show God our love is by obeying Him. Another is by spending time with Him.

3. What specific actions are parents called to take as they seek to teach their kids about God? See Deuteronomy 6:7–9.

*we are to talk about God inside our homes, while out walking, when we lie down, when we rise.*

Are you not sure where to begin? Again, I encourage you to check out Appendix 4 for my recommended resources. I find summer to be a great opportunity for regrouping. Our schedules slow and our time feels under my control again. Each spring, I take inventory on where I'd like to see my kids grow spiritually. I develop a plan for the summer in which they are each required to have "quiet time" of Bible reading/study/prayer before the day gets going. It's been a goal of mine that they would be comfortable opening their Bibles and navigating their way around them before high school, and our summers have helped a lot in that regard. When they are younger, I read aloud to them, and as they get older, I give them resources and have them do it independently. As I was growing up, my mom paid me to read one psalm and one chapter of Proverbs a day and had me journal something that I learned. This is likely when I started developing the habit of reading the Bible and journaling each day.

An easy way for kids to journal their prayers is to use the anacronym ACTS.

Adoration (write down something about God that you are thankful for)
Confession (write down anything you'd like God to forgive you for)
Thanksgiving (write down your blessings and thank God for them)
Supplication (write down what's worrying you and ask God for what you need)

Just for the record, I am not above bribing. As my kids have gotten older and at times been resistant to what I want them to read, I give them reading goals with rewards along the way. This has made a huge difference. Even if their reading is reluctant, I know the words are still going in.

4.  A.  What is God concerned will happen to His children in times of prosperity? See
Deuteronomy 6:10–12. *He is worried that His children will forget Him. And instead of appreciating all of their prosperity as having come from God, they will instead credit themselves.*

   B.  What are some blessings that God has given your family that you rarely give Him credit for in front of your kids? When is a time in your day that your family could incorporate a practice of gratitude toward God?

   *At our dining table — or bedtime prayers*

*Quiet your heart and enjoy His presence…Take time to reflect on all He has done.*

*"What we have heard and known;*
*things our ancestors have recounted to us.*
*We do not keep them from our children;*
*we count them to the next generation,*
*the praiseworthy deeds of the LORD and his strength.*
*the wonders that he performed.*
*God made a decree in Jacob,*
*established a law in Israel:*
*Which he commanded our ancestors,*
*they were to teach their children;*
*that the next generation might come to know,*
*children yet to be born*
*In turn they were to recount them to their children,*
*that they too might put their confidence in God,*
*and not forget God's deeds,*
*but keep his commandments." (Psalm 78:3–7)*

*This passage describes passing the baton of faith to the next generation—something we all have been asked to do. We don't always know what's going to make things "stick," especially since each child is unique. I asked my older kids what they can remember being most effective during the elementary school years and this is what they shared:*

- *Being prayed with when they went to bed*
- *Going to school Mass during the week*
- *Parents' passion and commitment to their faith and to each other*
- *Being reminded of God's strength when stories of the Bible were referred to during the day*
- *The kids' Christian music that was playing pretty much all the time*
- *Being challenged to make a "prayer space" at home*

*It's interesting to me that some of the things that I thought were great didn't make the list, and things that I hardly thought about at the time actually had a big impact. This reminds me that while we should do all we can to pass the baton of faith to our children, there comes a point when it is out of our hands and we need to trust that God is at work. He takes our efforts and infuses them with supernatural grace, for supernatural results, many of which we don't see for decades.*

*Dear Lord,*
*Help me to pay attention to the times when the enemy uses discouragement as a tool to keep me from prayer and action. May the eyes of my heart be enlightened so I might know what hope I've been called to.[69] I can have hope in any situation because of You. When my focus slips from You and centers on my own abilities, I feel deflated. But if I keep my eyes on You and remember that You are always at work, I remember that it's not all up to me. Help me to do my part. May I be faithful to have resources on hand for my kids. May I be wise and not allow my kids to be overscheduled so there's time for what's truly important. May I be patient and trust that "He who began a good work in [my child] will bring it to completion at the day of Jesus Christ" (Philippians 1:6). Amen.*

# Day Three
# THE MIDDLE SCHOOL YEARS (12–14)

The shift into the middle school years is a significant one. The problem is not that middle schoolers don't think. It's that they begin to think well. In an article titled "What Parents Should Know: Adolescents Are Like Lawyers," Professor Nancy Darling explains the cognitive gains made in these years. Middle schoolers can think about possibilities and abstract concepts, they can think about thinking, they can play one idea off another, and they can understand different points of view.[70] This cognitive development means

---

69  Paraphrase of Ephesians 1:18.

70  Nancy Darling, "What Parents Should Know: Adolescents Are Like Lawyers," September 9, 2010, https://www.psychologytoday.com/us/blog/thinking-about-kids/201009/what-parents-should-know-adolescents-are-lawyers.

middle schoolers aren't just going to accept things at face value. They'll question what's presented and develop their own opinions.

These cognitive advances make the middle school years a great time to teach kids about truth and lies. They are able to understand that when a point of view is presented to them, *they get to choose whether they embrace it* or look for another perspective. This is why the BLAZE program at Walking with Purpose focuses on the lies our culture feeds middle school girls. You'll want to check out those resources for your daughters. But for this lesson, I'm going to keep things more general, so it applies to sons as well.

You'll notice that today's lesson follows a different format. We'll focus on four lies middle schoolers need to recognize, reject, and replace with the truth. To start with, we'll explore what it feels like to believe the lie (spoiler alert: it feels pretty rotten). This helps kids to see why talking about truth and lies matters. Then we'll dig into Scripture to discover the truth. Finally, I'll give a little commentary on some ways you can discuss each lie with your child.

1.  **Lie 1:** God made a mistake when He made me.

    A.  How do you think believing this lie can be harmful to middle schoolers?

    *Self-esteem & self-worth are harmed. Mistake is equal to unloveable and that is antithesis of God.*

    Most middle schoolers struggle to feel comfortable in their own skin. Their bodies are changing, and most kids aren't happy with how they look. Friendships shift and what once seemed simple now feels complicated. Adolescents can quickly move from "I don't like what I look/feel like" to "There must be something wrong with me." Things become even more complex when gender identity and sexuality come into question. How do kids feel when they believe the lie that God made a mistake when He made them? They feel confused, anxious, and depressed instead of secure and confident.

    B.  What is the truth? See Ephesians 2:10 and Psalm 139:13–16.

    *We are God's workmanship created in Christ Jesus for good works*

    Ephesians 2:10 speaks of us as God's "workmanship," which is translated from the ancient Greek word *poiema*. The idea is that we are God's beautiful poem.[71]

---

71  David Guzik, "Study Guide for Ephesians 2," Blue Letter Bible (accessed March 26, 2021), https://www.blueletterbible.org/Comm/guzik_david/StudyGuide2017-Eph/Eph-2.cfm?a=1099010.

Psalm 139:13–16 reminds our kids that God knows them inside and out. He knows exactly how they were made because He was the sculptor. He has watched them grow and actually prepared every single day of their lives before they had even lived one day.

Core message: "When God made you, He thought about every detail of your appearance, your personality, your gender, your abilities, and your heart. The truth is that not only did God make you, you are His masterpiece. He looks at you and is thrilled with what He has made. No matter what other people have said to you, God is completely crazy about you. You are not an accident. Even if your parents didn't plan you, *God did*. He did not make a mistake when He made you."

2.  **Lie 2:** Athletic and attractive people are worth more.

   A.  How do you think believing this lie can be harmful to middle schoolers?

*That their own uniqueness of talents + abilities don't matter — That they will never matter and/or worth less than others.*

How kids feel if they believe the lie that athletic and attractive people are worth more depends. If they feel athletic and attractive, that can lead to pride or basing their identity on something that could ultimately be taken away. If they don't feel they measure up, it can lead to low self-esteem and even self-loathing. It can cause middle schoolers to hold back from taking healthy risks and trying new things because they don't want to stand out and be found wanting.

   B.  What is the truth? See 1 Samuel 16:7.

This verse is part of a passage of Scripture in which God sent a prophet to anoint the next king of Israel. The sons of a man named Jesse were paraded in front of the prophet, and with each one, God said, "No, this isn't the one." The prophet assumed God would choose the tallest and strongest one. But the one He chose to be king was in the pasture with the sheep—not even considered worthy to be brought to the prophet. What God said about Jesse's sons is what He still says today: the outward appearance is not what matters. As Venerable Archbishop Fulton Sheen said, "Beauty on the outside never gets into the soul, but beauty of the soul reflects itself on the face."[72]

---

72  Dominic Figueroa, "What Every Girl Should Really Know," Culture Project, May 28, 2019, https://thecultureproject.org/what-every-girl-should-really-know/.

Core message: "What matters most is nothing on your outside—your appearance or your abilities. Your worth comes from inside. You are amazing because God lives in you. That's what gives you dignity. If you define your worth by a role you play, an ability you have, or what you look like, you will end up being an insecure person, because all those things can be taken away from you. Your identity and worth are not things to be found, they are things that are given to you by God. He made you. He gets to decide what you are for and what you are worth. And what He says about you is you are worth *everything* to Him."

3. **Lie 3:** I need the approval of my friends to be happy.

   A. How do you think believing this lie can be harmful to middle schoolers?

The approval of the peer group becomes increasingly important in middle school. Peer pressure kicks in, and the smallest things can cause kids to be made fun of, left out, or ostracized. When kids need their friends' approval to be happy, their sense of well-being will yo-yo. They'll often feel that those around them are smarter, funnier, more athletic…just better. Social media exacerbates all this. The temptation for children to not be true to who they are is strong. The price they need to pay to stick to what they value can often not seem worth it.

   B. What is the truth? See Nehemiah 8:10 and 1 Corinthians 16:13–14.

Many things that lead us down the wrong path look harmless at first. If we aren't paying attention, we'll compromise and get sucked into some bad decisions. We are reminded in 1 Corinthians 16:13–14 that we need to stand firm in the faith. If we have made people's approval the most important thing to us, then we definitely won't stand firm in the faith; there will be just too many times when doing so will cause us to stand out and look different. But when we live for an audience of one—when we live in such a way that we bring God joy—we are filled with strength. And God never just keeps that joy for Himself; He pours it back into our hearts.

Core message: "Live for an audience of one. Ultimately, it is God's approval that matters. He knows what will truly bring you joy. God is not trying to spoil your fun; He wants to keep you on the path that will bring you what you most want in the end. If you decide that what God thinks of you is what really matters, it will change how you measure your day. Our tendency is to measure how good the day is by how people treat us and what they think of us. This means some days are good, many are not, and the whole thing is out of your control. But if you decide to measure your day by what God says matters, it's totally in your control. You can decide to live the way He asks you to (He asks you to love). At the end of the day, you can evaluate yourself against that. Ask yourself, 'Did I love well today?' If you did, then it was a good day. And if not, just ask God for forgiveness and the grace to do better tomorrow."

4. **Lie 4:** Following Jesus means I can't have any fun.

A. How do you think believing this lie can be harmful to middle schoolers?

Why would anyone want to follow Jesus if it looks like drudgery? We no longer live in a culture that expects us to attend church; it is one optional activity among many. Studies indicate that most young people decide that they are going to disengage from their Catholic faith at the age of thirteen—often before they actually stop going to Mass.[73] It's critical during these years that middle schoolers catch the vision that following Christ is the ultimate adventure.

B. What is the truth? See Psalm 37:4 and John 10:10.

*Psalms - When we find our delight in God, He gives us what our heart desires*
*John - The enemy is a thief who comes to steal & destroy; Jesus comes so we can have abundant life.*

The truth is, there are many things here on earth that bring us happiness, but they don't last. Happiness that stays forever is called joy, and we don't get it from our circumstances. We get it from God. But to trust God, we have to trust that He actually wants what is best for us. This can take time. Saint John Paul II says it so well: "It is Jesus that you seek when you dream of happiness; He is waiting for you when nothing else you find satisfies you."[74]

Core message: "When God tells us that we shouldn't do certain things, it isn't because He's a cosmic killjoy. It's because He knows what will truly bring us an abundant life. He knows what will really satisfy our hearts. God is inviting you on an adventure. The epic stories you read and the superhero films you see pale in comparison to the story He wants to write with your life."

---

73 Nicholas Wolfram Smith, "Study Shows Young Adults Leaving Church Start Down That Path at Age 13," *National Catholic Reporter*, December 11, 2018; https://www.ncronline.org/news/people/study-shows-young-adults-leaving-church-start-down-path-age-13.

74 John Paul II, "15th World Youth Day."

5.  How can you apply the lessons learned today?

*Quiet your heart and enjoy His presence…Trust that God loves your children even more than you do.*

*When I asked my son what he found helpful for his spiritual growth in middle school, he shared that the things he was exposed to (specifically, learning about the saints and reading a youth version of the Catechism) were great, but that it was incredibly important that he be allowed to question his faith. He appreciated adults engaging with him in discussions about it without being condescending. This allowed him to grow into a more mature understanding of his faith, which invariably led him closer to God. I share this because I think our tendency as moms is to panic when our kids start to question. We get so nervous that they're going to walk away from what we have taught them. But calm discussion, respectful listening, and good dialogue are far more effective than agitation and frantic argument. God loves our children even more than we do, and He is far more able than we are to watch over them. We can allow our kids to wrestle with questions without anxiety because we trust that God is in control.*

*Dear Lord,*

*Psalm 25:15 says, "My eyes are ever upon the Lord, who frees my feet from the snare." It's so easy for me to switch my focus from You over to all the obstacles I face. Help me to remember that when I focus on problems, fears, worries, and how hard everything is, everything else starts to fade away. That includes my trust in Your provision and protection. I pray that You would be at the center of my focus.*

*When I am ensnared by anxiety, please free me.*
*When I am ensnared by difficulties, please free me.*
*When I am enslaved by distress, please free me.*
*When I am enslaved by a negative attitude, please free me.*
*When I am enslaved by hopelessness, please free me.*

*When my child is ensnared by a lie, please free him/her.*
*When my child is ensnared by temptation, please free him/her.*
*When my child is ensnared by social media, please free him/her.*
*When my child is ensnared by the desire to be popular, please free him/her.*
*When my child is ensnared by discouragement, please free him/her.*

*Amen.*

# Day Four
## THE HIGH SCHOOL YEARS (14–18)

If you have a child in high school, you can attest that he or she is no longer a sponge that soaks up everything you say. The window of time when you could count on a captive audience has closed. But don't be discouraged. While your kids may not be listening to your words as well as before, they are observing your example. There is tremendous power in modeling the Christian life in a winsome way.

This truth reminds me of the film *Titanic*. I recently rewatched it and paid careful attention to the scene when the ship collides with the iceberg, causing it to sink. Interestingly, the iceberg didn't look terribly large, and the ship seemed formidable. In addition, once the crew saw the iceberg, they began to turn, so it wasn't a head-on collision. So why was the destruction so massive, taking the lives of more than fifteen hundred passengers and crew? The damage was so devastating because around 90 percent of an iceberg is below the surface. What you see on top is only a small bit of what is really there. It's what's below that makes it so strong.

We can draw a parallel to our lives. What other people see on the surface is only a small part of who we are. We have a life inside, an inner life that is the true source of our strength and our character. Everything is driven by what is below the surface of the water.

We live in a world that encourages us to put all our focus on the tip of the iceberg, but if we fall into this trap, our high school kids will notice our superficiality and lack of integrity. They sniff us out when we say one thing and do another, or when we put on a certain image in public and live very differently in private. So let's look at some ways we can model the Christian life authentically, making sure we give ample attention to what goes on below the surface.

1.  A.  Ephesians 3:14–19 tells us where we should begin: on our knees. Read this passage and note the vision Saint Paul casts regarding what is happening when we pray. *when we pray we are connecting with God who dwells in our hearts thru faith. This time in His presence Roots & grounds us in His love. We will be filled with the fullness of God.*

Without prayer, it is impossible to live the Christian life with authenticity. What is described in Ephesians 3:14–19 is a daily reset, an opportunity to renew your identity. During this time, you return to who you truly are: God's beloved daughter. You are reminded that it isn't all up to you—that you are an instrument of the Holy Spirit, but you don't have to carry the full weight of responsibility for others' actions. It provides an opportunity to think about any lies playing in your mind and replace them with the truth of what God says. We regain a sense of our identity, which helps us to head into the day clear about who we are and what matters most.

B. What additional insight do we gain from Psalm 51:6 regarding what goes on in "the inner man" when we pray intentionally? *Prayer offers us the opportunity to come clean with God. God meets us in our 'inward being' and teaches us wisdom*

C. We've discussed three fruits of prayer: reclaiming your identity by resting in God's love, coming clean with God through confession, and seeking God's wisdom. Which of these three are you in most need of today?

2. A. What are we told to seek in Colossians 3:1–2? *We are told to seek the things above. not on things of the earth.*

B. This verse is addressing what we value most. If someone were to observe you, what do you think he or she would assume matters most to you? If you have children, you might want to ask them what they see.

C. How is the temptation to compromise described in Romans 1:25? *It is to compromise /exchanging the truth about God for a lie and worshipping the creature rather than the Creator.*

In his excellent book on raising teens, *Age of Opportunity*, Paul David Tripp notes how this tendency to exchange worship and service for the Creator for worship and service for the created thing is a temptation for us all:

Yes, it's there in the life of the teenager who forsakes his convictions for the approval of his peers, but it is just as powerfully present in the adult who compromises family and spiritual priorities for professional success. The battle, as Paul understands it, is a heart battle, and it is dramatically important because what controls the heart will direct the life.[75]

3.  A.  Kids will be turned off by inauthentic faith, as well as by a religion that seems to suck all the joy out of life. If all kids see is dour obedience and duty fulfilled, they are going to run in the other direction. But what do we do if we don't *feel* love, joy, or peace? See CCC 736.

*They will crave love, joy, or peace. Allow for the Holy Spirit to work within us*

B.  Because the fruits of the Spirit find their source in the Holy Spirit rather than in us, we can tap into His limitless supply when we are lacking. Take some time to reflect on specific opportunities in your parenting or in your life where you can bear the fruits of the Spirit. Fill in the following blanks, then ask the Holy Spirit for help where you especially need it.

I can show love by _____.
I can show joy by _____.
I can show peace by _____.
I can show patience by _____.
I can show kindness by _____.
I can show goodness by _____.
I can show faithfulness by _____.
I can show gentleness by _____.
I can show self-control by _____.

Holy Spirit, please help me in this specific area:

I lack this fruit of the Spirit in my own strength, but I ask to draw upon Your limitless supply. Amen.

4.  What instruction is given to anyone who has a "flock" under his or her care in 1 Peter 5:2–3? How can you apply this verse to parenting?

*We are willingly to attend to the people that God has put under our care. Living by example — authentically.*

---

75  Paul David Tripp, *Age of Opportunity* (Phillipsburg, NJ: P&R, 2001), 16.

*Quiet your heart and enjoy His presence...Discover the power of confession.*

*In my years of parenting, I have found that it's been during the years of raising teens that I've been most aware of my need to confess my sin. It seems that my kids' mistakes bring out the worst in me. There's something about these particular trials that exposes my lack of patience, my desire to have a good reputation, and my dislike of discomfort. That craving for comfort can cause me to react with anger when my harmony, quiet, or peace is disrupted. My reaction reveals that I feel I have a right to these things. This spirit of entitlement can get in the way of me parenting well. So it's rare that I can't think of something to confess.*

*While you might expect this to discourage me, I have found that there are hidden blessings in this reality. Let me explain. When I sin in these ways, I hurt both my child and God. Both need to receive an apology. From my experience, when I confess my sin to my children, stating specifically what I have done wrong and then asking for forgiveness, something powerful happens in our relationship. They are quick to forgive, feel respected by the apology, and offer me a clean slate. It gives me a chance to remind them that while progress, not perfection, is what I expect of them, I really appreciate it when they offer the same to me.*

*But my kids aren't the only ones I have hurt. I need also to confess my sin to God. Something incredible about the sacrament of Reconciliation is the fact that we not only receive forgiveness, we receive a supernatural dose of grace to help us in the very area where we are struggling. This turbo boost of grace helps me fight the spiritual battle. When I am complacent and less aware of my need for this sacrament, I often leave grace on the shelf—grace I desperately need.*

*Dear Lord,*
*I am so grateful that every time I come to You needing forgiveness, You behave like the father of the prodigal son. You run to me with arms of mercy. May I be quick to turn to You, and may I then offer that same grace to those who have hurt me. May I be a woman characterized by humility. Amen.*

# Day Five
# THE YOUNG ADULT YEARS (18 AND BEYOND)

While these are years when our kids might not be living with us, our influence still matters. That being said, our approach needs to change. We need to take into account that while there is much life experience and knowledge that we have (and they don't), more often than not, the right thing to do will be to bite our tongues.

These are the years when we want to become experts at listening and asking good questions. Our goal is to get our young adults thinking about deeper things. All the while, we'll be wise to become powerful prayer warriors who never lose hope.

1. Read Luke 5:17–20. Describe the scene. For what reason did Jesus forgive the sins of the man? See Luke 5:20. *Because Jesus saw the faith in the actions of the man's friends who brought him to lifted him down to Jesus*

2. It is noteworthy that Jesus forgave the paralytic's sins not because of his personal confession, but because of the faith of those who carried him. Who would you like to lower through the roof to Jesus? Write his or her name here.

3. A. We are lowering our loved ones through the roof to Jesus when we intercede for them in prayer. There is something incredibly powerful about praying God's words back to Him. What does Isaiah 55:10–11 explain about God's Word? *God's word comes down from heaven to serve its purpose. God's words can speak something into being. His words create something out of nothing. God speaks to accomplish a purpose.*

   B. What does 1 John 5:14 promise regarding prayer? *If we ask for anything according to God's will, He hears us! He hears and He will respond.*

   In Isaiah 43:26, God said, "Put me in remembrance," and in Jeremiah 1:12, "I am watching over my word to perform it." He invites us to remind Him of His promises, asking Him to perform His Word in our lives and the lives of our loved ones.

4. You can turn just about any Bible verse into a prayer. Look up the following verses and rewrite each as a prayer for the person whose name you wrote in question two. The first one has been done for you as an example.

Jeremiah 24:7

I ask that You give my loved one a heart to know You, that You are the Lord, so that she will be one of Your people and You will be her God. May she return to You with her whole heart.

Ezekiel 11:19

*I pray that you give my loved one a new heart and a new spirit. That you will remove the heart of stone & make it a heart of flesh.*

Acts 26:18

*May you open my LO eyes and turn them from darkness to light; from the power of satan to you so that they may receive forgiveness of sins & a place among those sanctified by their faith in you.*

2 Timothy 2:25–26

John 6:44

Ephesians 3:18–19

During a time when I was especially worried about one of my children, I decided to pray every word of Scripture over his life. I bought a new Bible and began to read, underlining every verse with a promise to claim it for him. Then I wrote out a prayer claiming that promise in the margin. If there was an example to follow, I prayed for that. If there was an example of the opposite of what I wanted to see, I wrote down my prayer about that. Verse after verse, chapter after chapter, book after book, the Bible became filled with prayers for my child. The results were incredible. God's Word did not go out void—His purposes for my child's life were accomplished. And my own heart calmed at the same time. If you want to hear more about how to do this, check out "Truth with Handles Episode 3: Praying the Bible for Your Child" on the Walking with Purpose YouTube channel.

*Quiet your heart and enjoy His presence…God's Word will always achieve His purposes.*

*Praying the Word of God back to Him is a powerful form of prayer. Quoting God's Word out loud is one way we can wield the weapon of Scripture, because the enemy of our souls can hear us. When we speak self-defeating thoughts and worries, he hears them. He stores them away for later use. He uses them against us, and they ring true to us on some level because they were our thoughts and words to begin with. But instead of speaking defeat, fear, and worry, we can choose to speak God's Word. I encourage you to pray the following verses out loud, declaring their truth:*

*For I declare that "He who fears the Lord has a secure fortress, and for his children it will be a refuge" (Proverbs 14:26).*

*I declare that you "will contend with those who contend with us, and you will save our children" (Isaiah 49:25).*

*I declare that "not one word has failed of all your good promises" (1 Kings 8:56).*

*I declare that the eyes of the Lord are over the righteous and His ears are open to their prayers (1 Peter 3:12).*

*I declare that all my children shall be taught by the Lord; and great shall be my children's peace (Isaiah 54:13).*

*I declare that You have begun a good work in my loved one's life, and You will continue to complete it until the day of Jesus Christ (Philippians 1:6).*

*Amen.*

---

For additional material on how to effectively pass the baton of faith to this age group, see Appendix 5, "Connecting with the Spiritually Indifferent."

---

## Conclusion

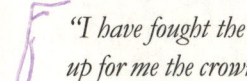

*"I have fought the good fight, I have finished the race, I have kept the faith. From now on there is laid up for me the crown of righteousness, which the Lord, the righteous judge, will award to me on that Day, and not only to me but also to all who have loved his appearing." (2 Timothy 4:7–8)*

At the end of our lives, we are going to want to be able to echo Saint Paul's words in 2 Timothy 4:7–8. We will want to have made the right choices that cause the Lord to welcome us as faithful servants. But I wonder if some of us, at the close of this lesson, are feeling discouraged. It could be that you feel you've come to this information too late. Each day's lesson might have caused you to feel regret for what you haven't done, rather than excitement for what the future holds. You might be thinking, *I tried; I did the best I could. I've got some regrets, but I can't go back and start the race all over again. Maybe things would be different if I had heard this earlier, but now? Now it's too late. I think this race is over.*

If that is where you are at, I want to respond to those feelings with an emphatic *no*. No, your race is not over. No, you are not finished yet. You are running a marathon. Do not get halfway through your race and then give up. No. Finish well. There will come a day when you can no longer run. Today is not that day.

What do you need to do to train for a marathon? One critical thing is to examine the course. Get the lay of the land. I grew up in Duluth, Minnesota, and Grandma's Marathon drew about ten thousand runners each year. The 26.2-mile course begins just outside Two Harbors and runs along the beautiful North Shore of Lake Superior. The terrain is relatively flat with some gently rolling hills, but at mile twenty-two, there's a large incline. Everyone in town knows it. It's brutal, and it's at the end. And if you don't know it's there, it can take you down, just before the finish line. But there's always a crowd gathered at that point—that's the place you tell your friends and family to show up to give you the encouragement you need to press on to the finish.

I won't deny it—we are facing an incline. There is a hill to climb, and it might seem insurmountable. But you are not alone. Lift your eyes to heaven with the words of Hebrews 12:1: "We are surrounded by so great a cloud of witnesses." The saints who have gone before us are watching us, cheering us on. They are shouting to us, "Don't give up! It is worth it. Just keep running!" So "let's lay aside every weight, and sin which clings so closely, and let us run with perseverance the race that is set before us." Let's ask for their prayers as we seek to pass the baton of faith to the next generation.

In the words of Venerable Fulton Sheen:

> Culture derives from woman—for had she not taught her children to talk, the great spiritual values of the world would not have passed from generation to generation. After nourishing the substance of the body to which she gave birth, she then nourishes the child with the substance of her mind. As guardian of the values of the spirit, as protectress of the morality of the young, she preserves culture, which deals with purposes and ends, while man upholds civilization, which deals only with means.[76]

The next generation needs every one of us engaging in this work. We need the mothers, the grandmothers, the aunts, the big sisters, the godmothers, the religious sisters, the neighbors, the volunteers, the teachers, the counselors…we need all hands on deck, forming an unbroken line of women who are willing to lean in and do what it takes to connect our children to Christ.

---

76  Fulton Sheen, *The World's First Love*, 2nd ed. (San Francisco: Ignatius Press, 2010), 188–9.

Spiritual growth can't be forced. Each child will choose for his- or herself whether a relationship with God will be embraced. We can't control this or make it happen, but together, we can smooth out the path toward Him.

*"Now to him who by the power at work within us is able to do far more abundantly than all we ask or think, to him be glory!" (Ephesians 3:20–21)*

## My Resolution

Examples:

1. I believe in the power of prayer. I commit to daily praying for the children I love, that they will experience a genuine and life-changing relationship with God.

2. I want to do a better job of asking deeper questions of the young adults I love. I will plan one-on-one time together, pitch some questions, and listen.

3. I don't have children living under my roof, but I still can influence the next generation. To that end, I will ask God to reveal to me a child who would benefit from my mentoring, and I will spend intentional time with him or her.

My Resolution:

## Catechism Clips

*CCC 736* By this power of the Spirit, God's children can bear much fruit. He who has grafted us onto the true vine will make us bear "the fruit of the Spirit: . . . love, joy, peace, patience, kindness, goodness, faithfulness, gentleness, self-control." "We live by the Spirit"; the more we renounce ourselves, the more we "walk by the Spirit."

> Through the Holy Spirit we are restored to paradise, led back to the Kingdom of heaven, and adopted as children, given confidence to call God "Father" and to share in Christ's grace, called children of light and given a share in eternal glory.

 NOTES

# Lesson 6

# PRIORITY 5: YOUR HOME

## Introduction

*"The ache for home lives in all of us. The safe place where we can go as we are and not be questioned."*[77]
—*Maya Angelou*

I've had many spells of homesickness over the years. Typically, I'd try to soothe myself by looking at houses online in the town where I grew up. I imagined what it would be like to move back to Duluth. Could I relive all the comforting memories? Would my desire to belong finally be satisfied if I could go back to those familiar people and places? Maybe you long for roots, too. Considering how rarely extended families stay close together as jobs and preferences transfer people to different parts of the country, I doubt that I am alone in these feelings.

I felt this homesickness most acutely when I lived in Mexico, in large measure because I was surrounded by the most beautiful display of family traditions that I'd ever seen. Families by and large stayed close geographically, with weekly gatherings for *comida* in which multiple generations stopped their activities and devoted the afternoon to each other. I admired it from the outside looking in because my family was far away.

During the three decades of my marriage, we have moved nine times. In every new place, I have yearned for what is around me to give me an immediate sense of grounding and security—to feel like home. In the broadest sense, I've wanted to live in a culture where people are cared for, justice prevails, and a good dose of joy is experienced. But what I found was that many things needed to be in place for that to occur, and most of them were beyond my power. This left me with a choice. I could focus on all the things I didn't like—things that made me feel out of control and discontented—or I could

---

77   Maya Angelou, *All God's Children Need Traveling Shoes* (New York: Random House, 1986), 196.

focus on the tremendous impact my simple household could make. I wanted home to be bestowed on me, but I needed to answer the call to create what I longed for.

*Home* wields a power for good or for ill, and as society at large needs more and more reform, there is an even greater need for our homes to be life-giving. This may seem an obvious point. What is perhaps less obvious is just what it takes to have that kind of a home. It demands something of us that goes beyond having a roof over our heads, takeout for dinner, and Netflix for entertainment.

The year 2020 is one that will be remembered for decades to come. It's the year we all were sent home. Worldwide lockdowns meant families were together, slowed to a pace most had never experienced before. Perhaps the biggest surprise was how good it felt, in spite of all the upheaval. Most of us agreed that we wouldn't want to live like that forever. But many were wistful as the pace of life returned to the pre-pandemic whirlwind.

Author Wendell Berry writes, "the world cannot be discovered by a journey of miles, no matter how long, but only by a spiritual journey, a journey of one inch, very arduous and humbling and joyful, by which we arrive at the ground at our own feet, and learn to be at home."[78] That is the goal of this lesson—for us to learn to be at home. It requires that we settle, take stock, and refocus. Only then will we be able to create the kind of home that allows those who cross the threshold to feel safe and known, ourselves included.

## Day One
## THE FIRST HOME

The first home in Scripture was a garden paradise. The people in this home had meaningful work, time for rest, and the pleasure of the best company: God Himself.

1. What did God give to man after He created him in His image and likeness? See Genesis 1:26..

   *Dominion over fish, birds, cattle and all the earth.*

The word translated *dominion* means to prevail against, to reign, to rule.[79] God was giving man the earth and asking him to take care of it in such a way that he would

---

78  Wendell Berry, *The Unforeseen Wilderness* (Emeryville, CA: Shoemaker Hoard, 2006), 43.

79  *Strong's Concordance*, s.v. "Radah," Bible Hub (accessed April 14, 2021), https://biblehub.com/hebrew/7287.htm.

prevail against anything that would destroy it, and to rule and reign in such a way that brought blessing.

2. A. How well did Adam and Eve do with that charge "to prevail against" anything that would destroy their garden paradise? See Genesis 3:1–7.

*They failed to prevail against the enemy Sin*

The serpent was a predator who entered their home, and instead of prevailing against him, Adam and Eve gave in. Sin entered their home, and things would never be the same. As is always the case, sin separated them from the goodness that God had planned for them.

But God did not give up on humankind. He didn't snatch back control, telling us that from here on out, He would be the one making every decision. He continued to task His children to rule and reign, prevailing against anything that would destroy the world He has given us.

One of the places He asks us to exercise dominion is in our homes. This is the domain He has entrusted to us. While there is much we cannot control outside our doors, we can create a tremendous amount of change within the walls of our homes. We have a God-given authority and the responsibility to prevail against anything that would destroy the people under our care.

Sometimes we fail to exercise this authority because we have abdicated responsibility. We have handed it over to the schools, or to religious education at our parish, or to sports coaches. Often we do this unintentionally, but the results are the same. Things that are important to us don't translate into our reality and we make the faulty assumption that there's nothing we can do about it. But having dominion means that you do not need permission from someone outside your home to do what you know is best for your family.

Other times we fail to exercise this authority because we are too busy trying to fix people and problems that are not under our dominion. We are messing around in someone else's garden. We are sharing our opinions or trying to control things in areas that are not our responsibility.

B. How effectively are you exercising your God-given authority in your home? Are you doing your best to prevail against anything that would destroy the goodness in your household? Is there anything you are tolerating under your roof that you know is dishonoring God? What holds you back from making the changes you know are needed?

C. Is there a "garden" that doesn't belong to you that you are tempted to step into and fix? Have you noticed how there is no peace in that process, and how rarely the change you want to see occurs? Issues with extended family often fall under this category.

3. What does Song of Solomon 2:15 tell us to "catch" in our vineyards? What will happen if we don't? *We are told to catch little foxes in our vineyards — otherwise, the vineyard will be spoiled.*

While a fox is a relatively small animal, it can do enormous damage to a vineyard. Foxes are meat eaters, but they also like fruit. In a vineyard, they will bite off the shoots, chew on the roots, and consume the grapes before they can be harvested.

"Foxes in the vineyard" are attitudes, problems, and decisions that seem small but actually destroy the fruit that we are trying to cultivate in our homes.

When author Gladys Hunt was asked, "What is home?" she replied, "My favorite definition is 'a safe place,' a place where one is free from attack, a place where one experiences secure relationships and affirmation. It's a place where people share and understand each other. Its relationships are nurturing. The people in it do not need to be perfect; instead, they need to be honest, loving, supportive, recognizing a common humanity that makes all of us vulnerable."[80]

This is the kind of environment we are tasked with creating. To create and maintain it will require prevailing against anything that would spoil it. Which "foxes in the vineyard" are keeping your home from being the safe place Gladys Hunt describes?

---

80  Gladys Hunt, *Honey for a Child's Heart: The Imaginative Use of Books in Family Life* (Grand Rapids, MI: Zondervan, 2010), 93.

4.  A.  When sin entered the Garden of Eden, Adam and Eve felt exposed and hid themselves. God went in search of them, and when He asked them what had happened, there was a common thread in both Adam's and Eve's responses. What was it? See Genesis 3:11–13.

    *Adam blamed the woman who blamed the serpent.*

    B.  These verses remind us that our natural tendency is to look for someone or something to blame outside ourselves when things go wrong. Read Psalm 101:2–3, and write the second part of verse 2 and the first part of verse 3 here.

    *I will walk with integrity in my house, I will not set anything that is bad before my eyes*

    C.  Instead of playing the blame game, let's take responsibility for our actions. Is there something we are setting before our eyes that needs to go? Is there a sin that needs to be confessed? If you feel ready and willing, write a prayer here expressing your commitment to walk with integrity of heart within your home. Be specific about what needs to change.

    Dear Lord,

---

*Quiet your heart and enjoy His presence…You have God-given authority.*

*"Behold, I have given you authority to tread upon serpents and scorpions, and over all the power of the enemy." (Luke 10:19)*

*Jesus spoke these words to seventy followers whom He had sent out as "lambs in the midst of wolves" (Luke 10:3). They were to spread the kingdom of God as they journeyed from town to town. Without question, there was resistance to their work, but "the seventy returned with joy, saying, 'Lord, even the demons are subject to us in your name!'" (Luke 10:17).*

*There is power in the name of Jesus. The authority you carry in your home ultimately comes from Him. God is the One who has tasked you with the important job of passing the faith to the next generation and creating a home that evangelizes. It is His power within you that gives you the courage and ability to draw a line across your threshold that says, "That may not enter." Whatever "that" may be, it will take persistence and determination to stick to your convictions. You won't necessarily be the popular one, or the fun one. You might even lose some friends. You have to decide whether paying that price is worth the end result.*

*In Luke 14:28, Jesus asked, "For which of you, desiring to build a tower, does not first sit down and count the cost, whether he has enough to complete it?" There is a cost to building a home that honors Christ. But the end result is the creation of a safe place, a garden of refuge.*

## Day Two
## IF THESE WALLS COULD SPEAK

Have you ever thought about the story being written within the walls of your home? Think of all the conversations that have taken place—some hasty and others so intentional that they have marked turning points in your life. Without a doubt, the words in our homes carry power, for good or for ill. "A word fitly spoken is like apples of gold in a setting of silver" (Proverbs 25:11). Offering the right word at the right time is like presenting a beautiful golden apple on a stunning silver platter. It is a delight for all and brings a sense of pleasure to the room. But even more important, such words have healing, strengthening, and restorative power. They can create before-and-after moments that offer critical guidance and even rescue.

1.  Read the following proverbs, noting what they have to say about the importance of our words.

    Proverbs 15:1


    How often do you use sarcasm, a raised voice, or insults when you are frustrated?


    Proverbs 19:11


    Are you able to let small things go, or does your anger get ignited quickly?


    Proverbs 21:9

Do you notice certain loved ones shutting down and withdrawing from you in conversation? Could that be because you are often argumentative, directive, or corrective? Is it possible that this wears people out and causes them to disengage?

2. It isn't only the content of our words that matters. Tone and accompanying facial expressions are also critical. If we want people in our homes to experience secure relationships of affirmation, we'll pay attention to all the ways in which we communicate with one another. This is an area where we often need help to know what it's like to be on the other side of us. We don't see our own expressions and often are blind to our tone. It can be very helpful (although vulnerable and humbling) to ask family members for feedback. With which loved ones do you think your expressions and tone might need some improvement? Did any of the proverbs in Question 1 cause you to reflect on your own behavior? If so, which ones? In what way?

3. Home is the place where we learn who we are. Children are wet cement, and what we communicate to them when they are young in terms of their identity takes hold. What do the following verses teach in terms of critical truths to know regarding identity?

John 1:12

Romans 8:16

2 Corinthians 5:17

Galatians 3:26

Galatians 4:7

These are key truths that we will want to speak of to our children, and if they can commit them to memory, so much the better. These truths are a stake in the ground, something that tethers us to an identity that is given, not discovered.

A plaque sits by my daughter's bed with words that echo the teachings of these verses. She has memorized it, and whenever she feels insecure, I ask her to recite it out loud. These words have truly made a difference in her life: "I am a daughter of the King. That makes me royalty. Nothing on the outside, but Christ on the inside, He is my identity."

This seems easier and more acceptable to do with children, but the adults in our lives need this more than we might realize. Our need for words of blessing and encouragement only increases with time. Do you feel like you would be just stating the obvious? Say it anyway. Over and over again. We never tire of hearing that we are good, loved, and a gift to those around us.

4.  The late Navigators Ministries staff member George Sanchez said, "Hold a crown a couple of inches above their heads and encourage them to grow into it."[81] This is a form of spiritual vision casting. When we were baptized, we were anointed priests, prophets, and kings. We can practice the gift of prophecy in our own homes by speaking words of future blessing. We can envision what our loved one would be like if he or she was fully surrendered and obedient to God. You can hold a crown above their heads by writing a letter or a text sharing what you appreciate about them. Draw attention to where they are making an effort. Think about their physical, mental, social, and spiritual qualities.

    Who would benefit from you holding a crown above his or her head? What are some of the good qualities you would like to draw attention to?

*Quiet your heart and enjoy His presence…Ask God to share His perspective.*

*"To love someone means to see him as God intended him." —Fyodor Dostoevsky*

*It doesn't take much for us to fall into the habit of looking at those closest to us through a pretty negative lens. The closer we are to someone, the more we're going to notice little idiosyncrasies and habits that we wish would go away. To counter this, I daily pray for the supernatural gift of prophecy—to be a*

---

81  Jean Fleming, *A Mother's Heart* (Colorado Springs: Nav Press, 1994), 149.

*supernatural encourager, able to see my husband's and children's flaws, but also who they could be, what they would be like, walking in their true identity as beloved sons and daughters of God. Reminding myself of the things that have hurt them helps me recognize when they are operating out of their brokenness. Perhaps something has triggered them during the day. Whatever is causing the current unpleasantness, I'm reminded that we are all the walking wounded, and a little extra care and an encouraging word go a long way.*

*Dear Lord,*
*Help me to see my loved ones through Your eyes. Help me to see how hard they try, instead of focusing on the ways they fall short of my expectations. May I pay attention to and comment on the ways they have grown over the years. Forgive me for the times I hold them to a standard of perfection that is impossible to reach. May our home be a place where grace reigns.*

*There is so much outside our door that tears down my family members. They each walk out and experience things in their day that erode their sense of self-worth. When they cross the threshold, coming home, they need to be rebuilt, not further torn down. We are told in 1 Thessalonians 5:11 to "encourage one another and build one another up." May my words do this in the relationships that matter most to me. When I am tempted to speak in a way that is angry or degrading, please "set a guard over my mouth, O Lord, keep watch over the door of my lips" (Psalm 141:3).*

*May my home be a place where identities are restored. Amen.*

# Day Three
## CREATING BEAUTY IN THE EVERYDAY

At Walking with Purpose, we often talk about the way beauty breaks down barriers. It disarms us, catches us by surprise, and draws us in. Creating an atmosphere of beauty ministers to people on the level of their senses, and wordlessly communicates that this is a place to lay down your load and soak up something good. When we take the time to set the table, place a cozy blanket near the couch, or put some flowers in a vase, it communicates the message, "You matter. I did this for you. You were worth the time it took to make this space welcoming and lovely."

A beautiful home isn't about fancy fixtures and designer decorating. It's about creating spaces that are nourishing to the spirit and healing to the heart. We read in Psalm 50:2, "Out of Zion, the perfection of beauty, God shines forth." One of the meanings of the word *Zion* is "stronghold or fortress," a place where God dwells.[82] It's a place of protection and beauty *because God is there.*

Can we catch this vision for our homes? If we will invite God to come in, He promises to infuse our homes with His own presence. Something beautiful will always result. And He invites us to collaborate in that creative process. So let's explore how, in partnership with God, we can create homes that provide a beautiful oasis for all who enter.

1.  A.  What do you learn about God and His desire for us in 1 Corinthians 14:33 and 14:40?

There is beauty in order. Far from limiting creativity, order calms us and gives us the space and clarity to think freely. An example of this comes from Saint Benedict and the monasteries he founded. The civilization of Rome was crumbling during Saint Benedict's lifetime, but instead of becoming paralyzed by discouragement, he chose to focus on what could be done within the walls of the monastery. The monastery helped to preserve the ancient learning and culture of Greece and Rome, and it innovated in the areas of art and science.

The lives of the friars are described in the excellent book *Theology of the Home:*

> Their lives, a balance of *ora et labora*, order and prayer, with highly structured days devoted to God, bore the fruit of God's love made visible in the material goods they produced. When the rest of the world was given over to panic, mayhem, fear and anxiety, their devotion to God, embodied in a rhythm of life marked by order, structure, and reverence, left a creative legacy that blossomed and endured.[83]

  B.  What are some practical projects you could tackle in your home to create more order? Is clutter limiting your ability to be creative? Would your home environment be improved if you chose to curate what's in your house instead of just accumulating more and more?

---

82  *Strong's Concordance*, s.v. "Tsiyyon," Bible Hub (accessed April 15, 2021), https://biblehub.com/hebrew/6726.htm.

83  Carrie Gress, Noelle Mering, and Megan Schrieber, *Theology of the Home: Finding the Eternal in the Everyday* (Charlotte, NC: Tan Books, 2019), 118.

2.  A.  One of the wonderful things about being Catholic is that all our senses are tended to. Woven into the fabric of our faith are things that we can touch, see, taste, hear, and smell. What do the following verses teach us about the role fragrance should have in the life of a Christian?

    2 Corinthians 2:14–15

    Ephesians 5:1–2

    B.  I am all for having scented candles throughout the house. I usually have one burning near the front door and one in the kitchen so that when anyone enters my home, they are greeted with a lovely aroma. But these verses are talking about a different kind of fragrance. The fragrant offering of Christ that we are to imitate is that of a pleasing sacrifice. This sweet-smelling aroma is what results when we give ourselves in love to others.[84] What might God be asking you to offer as a sweet sacrifice of love in your home?

3.  A.  One of the ways I love to create beauty in my home is by setting the table before I go to work. I love to use cloth napkins, candles, fresh flowers, and the good dishes. I don't believe in saving these things for special occasions because I think the ordinary days are actually the precious ones I'll look back on with the most nostalgia. As author Kurt Vonnegut wrote, "Enjoy the little things in life because one day you'll look back and realize they were the big things." But none of this will matter if I don't practice the principle taught in Proverbs 17:1. What is it?

    B.  What are your conversations during dinner like?

---

84  David Guzik, "Study Guide for Ephesians 5," Blue Letter Bible (accessed April 15, 2021), https://www.blueletterbible.org/Comm/guzik_david/StudyGuide2017-Eph/Eph-5.cfm?a=1102002.

Dinnertime is a wonderful opportunity for reconnection, but over the past three decades, family time at the dinner table has declined by more than 30 percent.[85] For many families, reclaiming this time feels like an insurmountable battle. But don't forget what we learned in Day One. *You have dominion and authority over your home.* Although it often feels like someone else is in charge of your family's schedule, that is actually a lie. True, there is a cost to swimming against the current. But what are we gaining with all our running around to sports and music practices? And what is the cost? What are we sacrificing? Is it worth it?

At our house, I have found that few things ground us so well as family meals. Something sacred happens around the dinner table. We are careful about what we talk about, making sure that everyone has a chance to share. We've found the simplest way to do this is to have everyone share their thorn (what was tough) and their rose (what was good) from the day. Others share their highs and lows. We also have bought sets of questions like Table Topics (available on Amazon), which provides great conversation starters. This isn't the time for nagging or correcting (we at least *try* to avoid this); it's for reconnecting and being reminded that what goes on outside our door matters far less than what goes on within our home.

4. One of the most important rooms in the house is the bedroom. This room above all should be an oasis. Technology of any sort will rob it of the peace it should provide. I'm also a big believer in the importance of making your bed each morning. I obviously couldn't find a Bible verse to support this, so you are free to ignore me completely, but I have found that when I leave my house each day, the state of my bedroom is the state of my mind. But far more important than the aesthetics of this room is the spirit and attitude that reigns there. What important truth do we learn about the bedroom from Ephesians 4:26–27?



Don't go to bed angry. I know—easier said than done. But do you know what helps enormously with this? Not reading emails or texts in the hours before bed. Not watching or reading the news before hitting the lights. Let's be honest, there's a lot out there that makes us angry, and much of that anger is justified. Ephesians 4:26 doesn't say we can't be angry, but it does tell us not to sin in our anger. And it also acknowledges that we are going to sleep best when we haven't gotten worked up right beforehand.

---

85 "The Benefits of the Family Table," American College of Pediatricians, February 2021, https://acpeds.org/position-statements/the-benefits-of-the-family-table.

So, what do you do when the problem hasn't come from technology, and instead it has to do with someone under your roof? This is where forgiveness and keeping short accounts comes in. There's a tremendous benefit to addressing things when they are small rather than letting them pile up.

*Quiet your heart and enjoy His presence…May your beauty permeate your home.*

*"The woman is at the heart of the home. Let us pray that we as women realize the reason for our existence: to love and be loved and through this love become instruments of peace in the world." —Saint Teresa of Calcutta*

*I believe the woman of the house sets the tone and attitude for the day. Her mood is caught by family members, and spreads throughout the house. Just as faith is caught more than taught, our irritable and critical spirits are contagious. We are called to be instruments of peace and beauty within our families. The beauty I am talking about is inner beauty, described in 1 Peter 3:4: "Let your adorning be the hidden person of the heart with the imperishable beauty of a gentle and quiet spirit, which in God's sight is very precious."*

*The way we spread peace and beauty in our homes is by embodying the love of God. The specifics of what that looks like are laid out in 1 Corinthians 13. The following prayer is based on that famous passage.*

*Dear Lord,*
*May I be patient and kind*
*Never jealous or boastful*
*May no arrogance or rudeness be found in me*
*Help me to not insist on my own way*
*Or be irritable or resentful*
*May I never rejoice at wrong*
*Instead, may I rejoice in what's good*
*May I bear all things*
*Help me to believe all things*
*May I hope in all things*
*And always endure.*
*Amen.*

*"Persevere in the exact fulfillment of the obligations of the moment. That work—humble, monotonous, small—is prayer expressed in action, which prepares you to receive the grace of that other work—great and broad and deep—of which you dream."*[86] *—Josemaría Escrivá*

---

86  Escrivá, *The Way*, 143.

# Day Four
## BUILDING A FRAMEWORK FOR HOME

1. A. What does a wise woman do according to Proverbs 14:1? How about a foolish one?


God used this verse to convict my heart early on in my marriage. I was celebrating yet another Mother's Day with Leo out of town on business. My four small children were giving me ample opportunity to practice motherhood, but not much time for being celebrated. I had expectations of how I wanted to be thanked, and I felt Leo had fallen short of the mark. I spent the day going over all the creative things he could have done to honor me even without being home, and ended with a bad attitude and a huge dose of discontent. As I crawled into bed, God brought this verse to mind. I had a choice. I could continue with my negative thoughts and self-pity, which was tearing down my home. Or I could choose to practice gratitude, which would build my house. I have found that this verse has the greatest application in terms of my thought life. I can certainly tear down my home with my actions and my words, but it's often what goes unseen by others that is the most destructive.

B. What is a way you can intentionally build your house? What is something you do that tears it down?


2. A. According to Proverbs 24:3–4, what builds a home, establishes it, and fills the rooms?


B. What do we learn about the virtues of wisdom, understanding, and knowledge from CCC 1831?


This means that while wisdom, understanding, and knowledge are perfectly possessed only by Jesus, He wants to share them with us as a gift. He knows this is what we need in order to live the life He calls us to. (God never asks something of us without equipping us for the task.) We receive these virtues as a gift when they are infused into us at Baptism and sealed within us at Confirmation. As with all gifts, they will grow stronger within us the more we practice them.

Knowledge is the process of gathering facts through study, research, and experience.

Understanding gives us insight into the very heart of things, especially what is necessary for spiritual maturity and salvation. Understanding helps us look at all the knowledge we have collected and then determine which parts of it are true. It allows us to extract meaning from information. Understanding brings what is true into focus.

Wisdom takes things one step further. It takes what we have learned through knowledge and understanding and allows us to apply it in our day-to-day lives. It's the ability to make the right moral and practical decisions, based on what God has said is true.

All three of these gifts are placed within us as a seed, but we have to cultivate them if they are going to grow to their greatest potential.

What can you do to grow in knowledge?


What can you do to grow in understanding?


What can you do to grow in wisdom?


Note: The answer key has some suggestions if you have trouble coming up with ideas.

3.  What daily rhythms would help bring wisdom, understanding, and knowledge to your home?

---

I have found that there are key points in my day that need special attention in terms of my routine. Morning, after school, and evening are my critical moments. When I let those time periods breeze by without being intentional about what I'm doing, I usually pay the price for it later. My morning and evening routines can be found in

Appendix 6. Take a look and make note of any that you might like to add into your own rhythm of life.

Having a set routine for my actions (one that I just *do*, that I don't need to think about) frees my mind to do the work of collecting knowledge, seeking understanding, and using wisdom in my decision-making.

4. If we pursue wisdom, understanding, and knowledge, there will be times when we feel that we might burst if we don't tell others what we have learned. We see a loved one about to make a poor decision and we know that if they would just listen to us, disaster could be avoided. This is a moment when we need to be careful. Before speaking, stop and pray. Ask the Holy Spirit if He wants you to say something, or if this is a lesson the person needs to learn on his or her own. What does Proverbs 31:26 tell us regarding how we should speak if the Holy Spirit leads us in that direction?

*Quiet your heart and enjoy His presence…He knows the best path for you to grow in wisdom.*

*"Wisdom is with the aged, and understanding in length of days." (Job 12:12)*

*One of my favorite passages of Scripture is found in Titus 2:3–5. In these verses, the older women are encouraged to "teach what is good, and so train the young women to love their husbands and children, to be sensible, chaste, domestic, kind…" Something powerful happens when wise older women choose to pour into the next generation of young women. For this to occur, two things are needed. The older women need to be willing to give of their time in this way, and the younger women need to both value the wisdom of those with more life experience and have the desire to build a home.*

*Betty Huizenga is a woman from Holland, Michigan, who decided to put this verse into action. She developed a program called Apples of Gold,[87] in which she trained older women to mentor younger women on the art of Christian homemaking. Betty gathered a group of mentors, mature followers of Christ who enjoyed cooking, setting a beautiful table, and the Bible. Young women who wanted to be cared for, appreciated, and pampered were invited to join. Everyone gathered first for a cooking lesson. The table was already beautifully set, providing inspiration and ideas women could transfer to their own homes. While the food cooked, the women did a Bible study lesson together, focusing on material that motivated them to be better wives and mothers. At the end, they all sat down at the lovely table for lunch and a time of informal sharing. These groups formed across the country, and the results were life-changing.*

---

87  "A word fitly spoken is like apples of gold in a setting of silver." (Proverbs 25:11)

*That was the call placed on Betty Huizenga's heart, and it was a big one. But don't minimize the impact one intentional relationship can have when an older woman opens her heart to a younger one.*

*If you find yourself in the older age group, who has God placed in your life who might benefit from you pouring into her life?*

*If you are in the younger age group, is there an older woman you admire who you believe could teach you something from her life experience?*

*In both cases, I encourage you to take the step of reaching out. Ask if you can meet for coffee. See if the Lord has something up His sleeve—if He is calling you to put Titus 2:3–5 into action in your life.*

## Day Five
## A SACRED SPACE FOR YOU

Saint Teresa Benedicta of the Cross described a woman as a shelter in which other souls can unfold.[88] This is a high and worthy calling and is exactly what we set out to do when we prioritize homemaking.

But I'd like to think back to my reflection in the introduction—to the ache we *all* have for home. Yes, we want to build a life-giving space for those we love, but we also long for that place of belonging and safety for ourselves. We, too, need shelter, a place where we can unfold, unravel, let down our guard, and roll the burden off our backs.

Is it possible to experience this ourselves while creating a home for those we love? Let's explore this together.

1.   A.   What does Jesus instruct us to do in Matthew 6:6?


The word translated "room" comes from the Greek word *tameion*, which means an inner room, a secret chamber, or a closet.[89] Jesus encourages us to go to this place, close the door, and meet with God, one-on-one. This is our starting point. This is where we are filled up, so that what is within us can overflow to those we love.

---

88   Sister Teresa Benedicta of the Cross, *The Collected Works of Edith Stein* (Washington, DC: ICS Publications, 2017), 132.

89   *Strong's Concordance*, s.v. "Tameion," Bible Hub (accessed April 20, 2021), https://biblehub.com/greek/5009.htm.

For some of us, the closed door is absolutely critical if we are going to have a restorative prayer time with the Lord. People who are helpers by nature often find that if someone else is in the room, they feel distracted by what the other person might need, even if he or she isn't saying a word. To ascertain if solitude is especially important for your prayer life, ask yourself the following questions:

If you are in a room with other people and someone asks you what you need, can you immediately come up with an answer? Or is your gut response "I don't know"?

If you are *alone* and can clear your head, are you able to figure out what it is that you need?

If you answered yes to these questions, then solitude in prayer (the closed door with no one but you and God in the room) is especially important.

B. What spot in your house can you claim as your inner room, your secret chamber? It doesn't need to be big—remember that the word could also be translated as *closet*. What can you do to make that space welcoming and cozy?

I like to keep some things in that spot—a scented candle, a soft blanket, a coaster for my mug, and a basket with my Bible, rosary, journal, and pen. That way I have everything I need when I sit down to pray. This space is holy ground. Even when I travel, I create these sacred spaces.

C. Are you in a season when it feels impossible to find time to be alone with God? What did Jesus have to do in order to meet with God in solitude? See Mark 1:35.

In my experience, there has been no substitute for setting my alarm to go off an hour before my first child wakes up. The exact time has varied over the years, but the need for an hour to myself has not changed. There were seasons in my life when this was impossible. When I had a baby and was up in the night with him or her, I needed all the sleep I could get. But when this was the case, I reserved the first pocket of quiet for the Lord. I never knew when it was going to come, but there was inevitably a moment in the day when I had time to grab my phone and scroll through social media or go and throw in a load of laundry. This was a decisive moment for me. Was I going to turn to a form of mindless relaxation or to doing something productive, or was I going to go directly to the source of grace and strength, the only One who could truly give me what I needed to get through my day? Choosing to turn first to Jesus always was the right choice. He then multiplied my time, making sure that I was able to do what was essential. He has never failed to do this.

2.  A.  What does Matthew 6:21 teach us about the heart?


    B.  What does 2 Corinthians 4:7 teach us about treasure?


    > The word translated "treasure" is a storehouse of precious things. Our bodies are the earthen vessels described in 2 Corinthians 4:7. What this means is that our heart is a storehouse of something precious: the very presence of God Himself and the grace He provides.

There will be times when you can't get to your inner room or secret chamber. Life is swirling around you and the chaos feels relentless. When this is your reality, be assured, there is a secret cloister within your heart, and you can always go there. Author Claire Dwyer describes this place in her book *This Present Paradise: A Spiritual Journey with St. Elizabeth of the Trinity*:

> [Saint Elizabeth of the Trinity] became aware that there was a cell in her soul, designed by the Holy Spirit, one where she could hold constant vigil, with a little sanctuary lamp burning continually in her heart…[she wrote] "You must build a little cell within your soul as I do. Remember that God is there and enter it from time to time; when you feel nervous or you're unhappy, quickly seek refuge there and tell the Master all about it."[90]

3.  A.  Has there been a time in your life when you have felt discontented with your "place"? Perhaps it was a house or a town you didn't want to live in. Maybe it was a job, a set of circumstances, or your vocation. Whatever the issue, you wanted out but had to stay. It could well be that this isn't something from the past—this is your current reality. Describe the place where you felt stuck, or feel stuck right now.

---

90  Claire Dwyer, *This Present Paradise: A Spiritual Journey with St. Elizabeth of the Trinity* (Manchester, NH: Sophia Institute Press, 2020), 33–4.

During a period when I felt trapped by undesirable circumstances, I encountered the story of an extraordinary man named Cardinal Francis Xavier Nguyen Van Thuan. When South Vietnam fell to Communist North Vietnam, he was arrested and imprisoned for thirteen years. He spent nine of those years in solitary confinement. This was a man who had devoted his life to pastoring his people, and the frustration of being separated from them when they needed him most was excruciating. One night in prison, he heard a voice telling him to discern between God and the works of God. While the works were good and important, they were not God Himself. As long as he chose God, he could trust that God was doing what was essential. In the Cardinal's own words:

> This light totally changed my way of thinking. When the Communists put me in the hold of the boat, the Hai-Phong, along with 1500 other prisoners and moved us to the North, I said to myself, "Here is my cathedral, here are the people God has given me to care for, here is my mission: to ensure the presence of God among these, my despairing, miserable brothers. It is God's will that I am here. I accept his will." And from that minute onwards, a new peace filled my heart and stayed with me for thirteen years.[91]

    B.   As you reflect on the testimony of Cardinal Francis Xavier Nguyen Van Thuan, how does it shift your perspective on your own unwanted circumstances? What might change for you if you said, "Here is my cathedral"?




4.   The ultimate perspective on our lives comes from the mouth of Jesus in John 14:1–3. Record these verses here:




Jesus has prepared a place for you. Your longings for perfection here on earth are God-given yearnings, meant to point you to your heavenly home.

Read Revelation 21:3–5 and describe what heaven will be like.

---

91   Joe Tremblay, "A Bishop Experiences God's Liberating Power," March 23, 2012, *Catholic News Agency*, https://www.catholicnewsagency.com/column/52080/a-bishop-experiences-gods-liberating-power.

*Quiet your heart and enjoy His presence…He wants to make His home in your heart.*

*"It is a fact that He creates places for us. Since Eden, He has carved out spaces and has hovered over our chaos to help us make rooms and homes, chapels and churches and places of pilgrimage that speak to us of something holy here and point to something holy beyond…"[92] —Claire Dwyer*

*On this pilgrimage to heaven, God provides rest stops along the way. Sometimes that's a place. Other times it's a person. Our loving Father knows that we need to catch our breath and refuel. But may we never mistake the road on the journey for our ultimate destination. We are moving forward, heading to a place where our yearnings will be satisfied and our hearts will become utterly settled and content. We'll be sheltered, safe, and at peace.*

*What this means is that no matter your circumstances, you are not stuck. You are not trapped. You are on a journey and are just passing through. The hard will not last forever. What has been prepared for you, if you could see it, would take your breath away. Just hold on, my friend. The Good Friday of this life will be followed by a resurrection beyond your wildest dreams.*

*Dear Lord,*
*Please help me to pay attention to the cloister within my heart. You wait for me there, every hour of the day. On this journey to heaven, You accompany me, step-by-step. I am never left alone. May I remember Your words: "Be strong and of good courage…Fear not, be not dismayed…God is with you. He will not fail you or forsake you" (1 Chronicles 28:20). Amen.*

## Conclusion

*"Unless the LORD builds the house, those who build it labor in vain.*
*Unless the LORD watches over the city, the watchman stays awake in vain.*
*It is in vain that you rise up early and go late to rest, eating the bread of anxious toil;*
*For he gives to his beloved sleep." (Psalm 127:1–2)*

As we reflect on all we have learned throughout this study, no doubt there is a list of things that you'd like to implement in your life. You've likely discovered some areas of your heart and life that need to be realigned. This is all a part of our journey to heaven. It's a constant recalibration as we discover new ways that God is offering us the opportunity to become more and more like Jesus.

On our pilgrimage to heaven, we'll need to hold two truths in tension. One is the importance of giving our all in our pursuit of Christ. He invites us to follow Him, and

---

92   Dwyer, *This Present Paradise*, 32.

that path isn't always an easy one. So there will unquestionably be many decisions we need to make, countless times when we'll need to strengthen our will to do what He asks instead of what we feel like. That is our part of the equation, and it is costly.

But another truth that is equally (if not more) important to grasp is the fact that the real power at work in this process is not ours, but His. Remember 2 Corinthians 4:7, from Day Five? We explored the treasure found in the cloister in our hearts. But the second part of that verse contains a critical teaching, the why behind it all: "We have this treasure in earthen vessels, to show that the transcendent power belongs to God and not to us."

Unless God is the one doing the building, our work is in vain. He doesn't ask us to behave as workhorses, never allowed to rest, valued for what we plow and produce. He asks us to behave as His children, utterly dependent on Him. Yes, we have been asked to create a home and keep our priorities in order. But God has provided all the help we need to do this without losing ourselves in the process.

We have the indwelling Holy Spirit, the tremendous power source, who reminds us of our true identity as beloved daughters. We have the Blessed Mother, who is our advocate and protector. She stands at the right hand of Jesus as the Queen of Heaven and ceaselessly prays for us. We have guardian angels who stand next to each one of us, protecting and shepherding us (CCC 336). We have "the great cloud of witnesses" (Hebrews 12:1), who are the saints in heaven. They know how hard life can be and are cheering us on. They are committed to interceding on our behalf with prayers filled with empathy and passion. We have the sacraments, which aren't just religious rituals meant to mark moments in our week or life. Each sacrament offers us an infusion of God's supernatural grace—the power to do things beyond our natural ability. What a tremendous privilege it is to be Catholic.

God has not left us alone. He didn't toss us a to-do list and then return to heaven. He made sure that we have everything we need. We are surrounded, sheltered, provided for, treasured, and protected by God Himself.

*"His divine power has granted to us all things that pertain to life and godliness, through the knowledge of him who called us to his own glory and excellence, by which he has granted to us his precious and very great promises." (2 Peter 1:3–4)*

# My Resolution

Examples:

1. I have identified something in my home that I know is not for the good of my family. I will exercise my God-given authority and make the necessary changes. I will not waste my time floundering with hesitation, doubt, or self-consciousness.

2. I commit to creating beauty in the everyday by setting the table in the morning and committing to technology-free, face-to-face family dinners.

3. I need a sacred space in my home, a place where I can retreat. I will create this corner for prayer, close my door, and daily meet with God there.

My Resolution:

# Catechism Clips

*CCC 336* From its beginning until death, human life is surrounded by their watchful care and intercession. "Beside each believer stands an angel as protector and shepherd leading him to life." Already here on earth the Christian life shares by faith in the blessed company of angels and men united in God.

*CCC 1831* The seven *gifts* of the Holy Spirit are wisdom, understanding, counsel, fortitude, knowledge, piety, and fear of the Lord. They belong in their fullness to Christ, Son of David. They complete and perfect the virtues of those who receive them. They make the faithful docile in readily obeying divine inspirations.

> Let your good spirit lead me on a level path.

> For all who are led by the Spirit of God are sons of God...If children, then heirs, heirs of God and fellow heirs with Christ.

Dec 1st hospitality
Dec 8th Fr Sam lunch
Dec 17th 6pm Mass.

# Lesson 7

# Priority 6: The World Outside

## Introduction

From the time I was young, my greatest ambition was to be a wife and mother. This is recorded for posterity on a VHS tape of a beauty pageant my childhood best friend and I put together for our seventh-grade friends. We paraded in our evening gowns and swimsuits, rocked our talent performances, and offered interviews. My talent was lip-synching Amy Grant's song "El Shaddai," and my interview captured my dream of raising a bunch of children. It's a priceless collection of 1980s preteen awkwardness and a recording of our plans for the future.

I wanted to grow up to be a soccer mom, one of my friends wanted to be a professional cheerleader, another a lawyer, another a doctor. When it all came down to it, things turned out differently than most of us had planned. Some of my friends wish they could stay home with kids but need to work. Others feel pressure to get their money's worth from an expensive college education with a subsequent career. Many women I deeply respect have pursued careers that have required their steady attention and commitment of time. Some had children, others didn't.

But I wanted to be a mom more than anything, and never felt "less than" for not having another career. My transition from full-time homemaker to working full time in ministry happened gradually. Bit by bit, the hours increased. Perhaps this is why when I was working thirty hours a week, I still referred to myself as a stay-at-home mom. Since that's where my office was, I figured the title still applied. But it failed to take into account that in working that many hours a week my life had drastically changed. I continued to hold myself to the same standards that I had lived up to when my days were less committed to people outside my immediate family. This was obviously a recipe for disaster. I needed to get realistic about what was on my plate and learn to say a lot of no's in order to say the best yes. Yes, my heart was at home, but a tremendous amount of my time and energy was being spent on the outside world.

Tending to the first five priorities—God, our hearts, our marriages, our children, and our homes—takes a boatload of time. But as we know from experience, there's more to life than what goes on inside our homes. We have other relationships and responsibilities, and 71 percent of women with kids under eighteen are working outside the home.[93]

It has been said that work-life balance is a myth, and if we pursue it, we'll drive ourselves crazy. A friend of mine talks about her work-life *rhythm*, and I like that description. There isn't a formula that makes everything work perfectly when there are so many variables at play. But as we look at the various parts of our lives that are outside our homes, we can learn some principles from Scripture that help keep the crazy at bay.

# Day One
## EXTENDED FAMILY

One of my favorite books is *Hannah Coulter*, by Wendell Berry. The protagonist, Hannah, describes love as "a great room with a lot of doors, where we are invited to knock and come in. Though it contains all the world, the sun, moon, and stars, it is so small as to be also in our hearts."[94] She explains that we stand in this room during our lives, and people come and go through the doors, filling the space with their presence and love.

This led me to think of all the people who have come through those doors in my life, and which ones have stayed. I think of my parents, grandparents, treasured aunts and uncles. Each brought love that surrounded me, encircled me. While many of them have left that room in some sense, I still feel them there. Their love remains. It's tangible. My sister came through another door, and a few friends would qualify, too. Then Leo came, and each one of my children.

I think it's such a beautiful picture, this room that holds our most precious people. We are back together in that room when in our tenderness we remember it all again.[95] I feel I carry each one of these precious people within me, my mother most of all. It's her voice

---

93  "Mothers Are Working Outside the Home," February 2008, National Women's Law Center, https://www.nwlc.org/wp-content/uploads/2015/08/WorkingMothersMarch2008.pdf.

94  Wendell Berry, *Hannah Coulter* (Berkeley, CA: Counterpoint Press, 2004), 51.

95  Berry, *Hannah Coulter*, 52.

that is in my head, guiding me toward the right decisions, encouraging me to persevere when I feel like quitting, helping me to value the things that truly matter.

1. Think about this great room of love in your heart. Who has entered it? Who has left? Who has stayed? Which person do you carry within you most of all?

There is no question that our family of origin and extended family have a tremendous impact on our lives. Sometimes what they have brought to us has been life-giving, other times it has been damaging, and most often it is a mixed bag. Even when we are trying our best to love well, we all fall short of the mark. The hurt that abounds in families is evidence of this. It can be hard to unravel the role that extended family should play in our lives when we are adults. The Bible gives us some guidelines that can be helpful.

2. A. What do we learn from Genesis 2:24 regarding what should happen when we marry?

*We leave our mother & father and the man & woman shall live as one.*

We run into a lot of difficulty when we ignore this instruction. The primary relationship needs to become that of the new husband and wife. When the strings to parents are held too tight, their expectations can cause feelings of guilt and undermine the couple's decision-making and unity. This process is described in the book *Boundaries*:

> A common sign of a lack of boundaries with the family of origin: the spouse feels like he gets leftovers. He feels as if his mate's real allegiance is to her parents. This spouse hasn't completed the "leaving before cleaving" process; she has a boundary problem. God has designed the process whereby a "Man shall leave his father and his mother and shall cleave to his wife; and they shall become one flesh" (Gen. 2:24 NASB). The Hebrew word for "leave" comes from a root word that means to "loosen," or to relinquish or forsake. For marriage to work, the spouse needs to loosen her ties with her family of origin and forge a new one with the new family she is creating through marriage.[96]

B. Can you identify areas in your own life where you need to set clear boundaries with extended family?

---

[96] Henry Cloud and John Townsend, *Boundaries* (Grand Rapids, MI: Zondervan, 1992), 131.

3.  A.  This verse is not teaching that we shouldn't have a relationship with our extended family. But that relationship changes when we move from childhood to adulthood. What do the following verses teach about the parent-child relationship?

Colossians 3:20  *Children must obey their parents.*

Exodus 20:12  *We are to honor our mother & father*

B.  Children are to obey their parents, but when we transition to adulthood, there is a shift. We are no longer required to *obey* our parents; we are to _honor_ them. This means we communicate with them, pray for them, and forgive them. What do the following verses teach about honoring parents? (Note: Some translations will use the phrase "hoary head," which means "white or gray-haired, aged.")

Leviticus 19:32  *You shall rise up before the gray head and honor the face of an old man, and you shall fear your God : I am the Lord.*

Proverbs 16:31  *A gray head is a crown of glory; it is gained in a righteous life*

Proverbs 23:22  *'Listen to your father who begot you and your mother when she is old*

1 Timothy 5:8  *If anyone does not provide for his relatives, and especially for his own family, he has disowned the faith & worse than an unbeliever -*

4.  But how do we respond when our parents are dishonorable? Note any insights gained from the following verses.

Psalm 27:10  *If or when your father or mother forsake you - the Lord promises to take care of you - (Hurt, disappointment, abuse, neglect or abandon)*

Psalm 68:5–6  *God is the Father of the fatherless & protector of widows. He gives the desolate a home to dwell in.*

Even if you are in an extreme situation in which you cannot be in communication with your parents, you can always honor them by faithfully praying for and forgiving them.

5.  Another dynamic at play is relationships with adult siblings. We easily return to childhood roles and patterns of behavior, and sibling rivalry and jealousy can last long into adulthood. What guidance does Philippians 2:3–4 give in this regard, and how can you apply it to your own life?

*Do nothing from selfishness or conceit, but in humility count others as better than yourself. Let each of you not only look to his own interests but to the interests of others.*

*Quiet your heart and enjoy His presence…He is the perfect Father.*

*Why do we so easily fall into old family patterns of behavior that we know hurt us? They are like well-worn ruts in the road. For our most formative years, it was the way we had to live in order to survive. Again, the book* Boundaries *is enlightening:*

> *The patterns you learn at home growing up are continued into adulthood with the same players: lack of consequences for irresponsible behavior, lack of confrontation, lack of limits, taking responsibility for others instead of yourself, giving out of compulsion and resentment, envy, passivity, and secrecy. These patterns are not new, they have just never been confronted and repented of.*

> *These patterns run deep. Your family members are the ones you learned to organize your life around, so they are able to send you back to old patterns by their very presence. You begin to act automatically out of memory instead of growth. To change, you must identify these "sins of the family" and turn from them.*[97]

*We won't break out of unhealthy patterns of behavior until we recognize that they fall short of what God is asking of us and that they are hurting us. The first step on the road to freedom is confession. This will help prevent us from justifying our actions or minimizing their negative consequences.*

*Dear Lord,*
*Please help me to identify harmful patterns of behavior that I have carried from my family of origin into adulthood. Help me to hold two truths in tension:*

1.  *My parents were doing the best they could. They, too, were dealing with baggage from their own childhoods.*

---

97  Cloud and Townsend, *Boundaries*, 137.

2. *Even though they tried, there were still areas of my life where the love I needed was not the love I received. This led to behaviors and coping mechanisms that were harmful.*

*I forgive my parents for the pain this has caused me. Forgiveness is a decision, which may or may not be accompanied by feelings. I am saying the words, even if my feelings are conflicting. I ask You to take care of my emotions. I do not want a root of bitterness to grow in my heart—I want to be free. So I forgive, and hand over to You the debt I feel I was owed. I ask You to take care of it all.*

*I also confess the patterns that I have perpetuated and commit to changing the way I behave. Please give me the strength to do this. Amen.*

# Day Two
## LIFE-GIVING FRIENDSHIPS

*"In friendship…we think we have chosen our peers. In reality a few years' difference in the dates of our births, a few more miles between certain houses, the choice of one university instead of another…the accident of a topic being raised or not raised at a first meeting—any of these chances might have kept us apart. But, for a Christian, there are, strictly speaking no chances. A secret master of ceremonies has been at work. Christ, who said to the disciples, 'Ye have not chosen me, but I have chosen you,' can truly say to every group of Christian friends, 'Ye have not chosen one another but I have chosen you for one another.' The friendship is not a reward for our discriminating and good taste in finding one another out. It is the instrument by which God reveals to each of us the beauties of others."[98]* —C. S. Lewis

1.  A.  What do the following verses say we should look for in a friend?

    Proverbs 13:20 We should look for wisdom b/c Those who walk w/ the wise become wise, Those who walk with fools become fools

    Proverbs 18:24 We should look for loyalty in our friends

    Proverbs 22:24–25 We should pay attention to friend who is quick to anger as we can start to reflect that trait.

    1 Corinthians 15:33 We should look for good character in a friend.

---

[98] C. S. Lewis, *The Four Loves* (San Francisco: HarperOne, 2017), 114.

B.  Do your closest friends reflect the character you want to see in yourself?

2.  A.  Friendship doesn't always come easily. Even if we've had a season of good friendship, a move or major life change can disrupt that. So what do we do when we realize we need to find new friends? Read 1 Peter 4:8–10 and record any ideas you find that would help in the search for a good friend.

*Above all, keep your love for one another constant. Because love covers a large amount of sins. Use your gift to serve one another as good stewards of grace.*

I have found that one of the best ways to make a friend is to look for ways that I can serve in my church, kids' school, or community. We all are using our gifts to serve others, and this work not only keeps our hands busy, it also keeps some of the awkwardness of early interactions away. We get a chance to observe one another and build some common memories without feeling it's too intense.

Hospitality is also important. There's something intimate about allowing someone into your home—it takes a relationship to a new level because you're revealing something new about yourself. There's an element of vulnerability at play, a key ingredient for good friendship. I want to encourage you not to wait until your house is perfect or in better shape before having someone over. We all have messes at home, and when you allow me to see yours, I don't judge you, I relax.

Do you feel like you are always the one who has to initiate, and is this getting on your nerves? There's no doubt that it's really satisfying when a friend pursues you, but if we sit around and wait to be invited, we could be waiting a really long time. How much better to just recognize that some people are initiators by nature, and if that's you, it really is just a text or phone call that's needed to get the ball rolling? Don't overthink it. Don't assume that you aren't getting invited because no one likes you. The truth is, most people are so wrapped up in their own lives that they just aren't thinking about much else.

B.  What do we see friends doing in Ecclesiastes 4:9–10?

*They are helping each other up.*

Who do you see needing to be helped up? Where can you show up and offer comfort or practical help? Friendship is often born where need and compassion intersect.

3.  A.  What role should our words play in our friendships? See 1 Thessalonians 5:11.

*We are to encourage one another and build each other up*

To do this well, we need to truly listen, then speak specifically about the good we see in our friends. As Dale Carnegie said in his classic book, *How to Win Friends and Influence People*, "You can make more friends in two months by becoming interested in other people than you can in two years by trying to get other people interested in you."[99]

B.  But sometimes, what we need most is simply the presence of a friend. Henri Nouwen wrote of this in his book *Out of Solitude*:

> When we honestly ask ourselves which persons in our lives mean the most to us, we often find that it is those who, instead of giving advice, solutions, or cures, have chosen rather to share our pain and touch our wounds with a warm and tender hand. The friend who can be silent with us in a moment of despair or confusion, who can stay with us in an hour of grief and bereavement, who can tolerate not knowing, not curing, not healing and face with us the reality of our powerlessness, that is a friend who cares.[100]

Can you think of a time in your life when your friend's silence meant more than her words?

*Sheila Dwyer when I was sick.*

4.  Ephesians 4:15 encourages us to speak the truth in love. If we are to do this, there will be times when our words don't feel very encouraging. What does Proverbs 27:6 say about this in regard to friendship?

*Faithful are the wounds of a friend.*

This verse says that wounds from a friend can be trusted. But this is true only if the friend truly desires your good. The motive behind her truth-telling matters. If this is a friend who loves you and wants what is best for you, her honesty might be the greatest gift she could give you.

---

99  Dale Carnegie, *How to Win Friends and Influence People* (New York: Simon & Shuster, 2010), 78.

100  Henri Nouwen, *Out of Solitude: Three Meditations on the Christian Life* (Notre Dame, IN: Ave Maria Press, 2004), 37.

*Quiet your heart and enjoy His presence…He'll help you love as Jesus loved.*

*"Let us consider how to stir up one another to love and good works, not neglecting to meet together, as is the habit of some, but encouraging one another." (Hebrews 10:24–25)*

*The book of Hebrews reminds us of the example Jesus set for us, running His race of life with endurance. Along the way, He gathered a group of close friends, and invested the majority of His time in them. He chose them carefully. Luke 6:12–13 says that He spent an entire night in prayer, "and when it was day, he called his disciples and chose from them twelve, whom he named apostles."*

*In his classic work,* Spiritual Friendship, *St. Aelred of Rivault describes three kinds of friendship: the carnal, the worldly and the spiritual. In his words, "The carnal is created by a conspiracy in vice, the worldly is enkindled by hope of gain, and the spiritual is cemented among the righteous by a likeness of lifestyles and interests."[101] With each of these types of friendship, the two friends both love something in particular. They might share a love of drinking to excess, or of getting ahead in the world through accomplishments. They might share a love of spiritual things, and as a result, both pursue growth in that regard. St. Aelred teaches that the worthiness of the object of love determines the quality of the friendship. As you think of your own friendships, can you identify the common love you share with certain friends? Is it love of a vice? Is it the pursuit of something worldly? Or is it a mutual pursuit of a growth in holiness because of a love of God?*

*Looking at the life of Christ, we are reminded of how important it is to intentionally run life's race with carefully chosen friends who will encourage us to grow in the right directions. A friend who stirs you up to love the right things—whose advice when you are frustrated is not to give up, rather to press closer to the Lord—is a true treasure. This requires an investment of time. It's always a temptation to "neglect to meet together" because our schedules are so often jam-packed. But our friendships will only flourish if we prioritize them.*

*Dear Lord,*
*I pray You would lead me to rich friendship and community, right where I am. May I not let laziness or preconceptions keep me from showing up and investing my time in others. May I surrender my idea of what my friends should be like so that I can have friendships rooted in Christ. May I learn to make meeting and getting together with people light and fun instead of full of heavy pressure. Help me to run my race with other women who are following after You. May my friends inspire me to remain faithful to You. Amen.*

---

Note: If you would like to delve more into the topic of friendship, I recommend the WWP six-lesson Bible Study *Reclaiming Friendship*, by Mallory Smyth, available in our store at www.walkingwithpurpose.com.

---

101  Aelred of Rivault, *Life-Giving Friendship* (Collegeville, MN: Liturgical Press, 2010), 62.

# Day Three
## PURSUING A WORK-LIFE RHYTHM

In the book *When Work and Family Collide*, Pastor Andy Stanley asks the reader to imagine a friend walking up and asking for a favor. The friend hands you a rock and asks you to stand with it until he returns. He promises to come back soon and retrieve it. The rock is heavy, but you're a trouper. Plus, you love your friend and gave your word. The hours go by, though, and your arms are starting to ache. Finally, the friend swings into the driveway, and your relief is palpable. But he doesn't take the rock back and instead asks you to keep holding it for just a bit longer. He just needs to run one more errand…and off he goes.

Hours later, another car pulls into the driveway, but it's not your friend. It's someone delivering the message that your friend was delayed but will be there soon. More hours go by. Your grip on the rock is starting to slip. You're trying to hold on to it, but your arms are hurting too much and finally the rock falls from your grip. Just at that moment, your friend shows up and asks, "What happened? Did it slip? Did someone knock it out of your hands? Did you change your mind?" He wonders why you *suddenly* dropped the rock, but you know it was a long time coming.[102]

Maybe you relate to this story because you've been the one left holding the rock. Maybe you are the one who has been asking your family to give you grace while you enter yet another week of working more hours than you should. Either way, we often find that there is just not enough time to do all that is needed at both home and work. So, what can help us with this dilemma?

1. Read Genesis 2:15, 3:3–6, and 3:17–18, noting what each verse is about, and the order in which these things take place. *The Lord put man in the garden to work + take care of it. After the fall of man, sin enters the world and then the fall being the consequence. B/c of sin, work is going to be difficult. The command to work comes before the fall + before the curse.*

   The point I am making is that before sin entered the world, man and work peacefully coexisted. But after the fall, the order of things was disrupted. Work itself is not the problem—in fact, we can see that work was a part of God's original plan. But sin has disrupted the work-life balance. Most of us feel these effects daily.

---

102 Andy Stanley, *When Work and Family Collide* (Colorado Springs: Multnomah, 2011), 38–9.

2. Two attitudes toward work are described in Ecclesiastes 4:6 and Proverbs 6:10–11. Read both verses and note the two extremes that are to be avoided.

   Ecclesiastes 4:6 *2 hands full of toil, but it isn't sufficient, it is striving after the wind. You never get there, it's never enough*

   Proverbs 6:10–11 *This person wants to nap, needs to take another break, and fails to do the work required.*

   Ecclesiastes 4:6 is aimed at the workaholic and paints a picture of a person who works too much. She spins and toils, constantly striving to do more and accomplish more. She might work nonstop, but it is never enough. She keeps asking her family to "hold the rock" but never pulls in the driveway to bring an end to the waiting. In other words, one season of intensity just bleeds into the next. Proverbs 6:10–11 is aimed at a person who values her comfort above all. She avoids getting down to business—she fails to do what duty calls for in that moment. Both extremes are easy to fall into, and we tend toward one or the other, depending on our personalities, work ethic, and family of origin.

3. A. What advice does Solomon give in Proverbs 15:16?

   *It is better to have a little with fear of the Lord than to have great wealth with turmoil & trouble.*

   B. What exactly are we working for? Is it possible that if we grew in contentment, we would be willing to work fewer hours? Read the following verses, noting anything that applies to the discussion of the role work plays in our lives.

   Psalm 127:2

   Proverbs 23:4

   1 Timothy 6:9–10

   Hebrews 13:5

4. Sometimes we work too much because we want a better standard of life. But often, we work so hard because we are trying to gain approval through our achievements. What does Galatians 1:10 say about this? *Do I pursue men or God?*

All too often, we are seeking approval in the workplace because of our need for affirmation. We don't verbalize this, and at first glance many of us would deny that this is our motivation. But is it possible that you are working so hard because you feel OK only if you are performing at a certain standard? What are you afraid you will lose if you cut back on work hours? Be specific. Is it a relationship? A perk? An opportunity? Someone's approval?

*Quiet your heart and enjoy His presence…Invite God's creativity into your problems.*

*Andy Stanley moves on from the rock illustration to make the point that because of our limited time, we are going to have to cheat somewhere. It will either be with our families or in the workplace. Why? Because it's impossible to fulfill all expectations in both those arenas. Stanley advocates choosing to cheat at work.*

*By this, he is not suggesting that we be dishonest or give our employers less than our best. But he recommends taking an honest look at our schedules to see if we are loving our families with our hearts but not our schedules. He writes, "In the world of relationships, we live with the illusion that good intentions—the desires of our heart—somehow heal the wounds we've created with our absences and mis-prioritization."[103]*

*It takes a tremendous amount of courage to do this if you tend toward working too much, but would you be willing to ask your spouse or child, "What change would you most like me to make in regard to my schedule?"*

*The next step is getting honest at work about what your nonnegotiables are. Is it being home by a certain time? Is it not taking phone calls in the evening? Whatever it is, it feels risky to set those limits, precisely because it involves risk. There are people in your life who will not affirm this decision. But it will deliver a strong message to your family regarding your true priorities. And it might prevent the rock from crushing down and damaging hearts and lives in the process.*

*Dear Lord,*
*I know that what my family wants more than anything is to feel that they are my priority. When I say one thing and do another, when I ask them to just keep waiting a little longer with the rock in their hands, I am eroding my most important relationships. I confess that more often than I would care to admit, I have sent my family the message, "You are important, but right now, something else is more important."*

---

103 Stanley, *When Work and Family Collide*, 28.

We are more than our work.

*Help me to have the courage to ask my family how I am doing in this regard. If changes need to be made, help me to make the decision to do whatever it takes to prioritize my family. Please grant me favor with my employer. Help us to be creative with the best way for me to serve my workplace without compromising my home. Amen.*

## Day Four
## YOUR MISSION FIELD IS WHERE YOU ARE

*Blossom where you are planted!*

It's easy to think about a job as something that we do to bring home a paycheck. But whether we work for the Church or in ministry, our places of work are holy ground. These are the locations where God has sent us out on a mission. No matter where we work or volunteer, we are coming into contact with souls that matter greatly to God. You may be the only Bible that those people ever read.

1.  What instructions are given regarding the way we are to work in Colossians 3:23?

No matter what we do, we are serving Jesus. This means that we want to give our very best to any task. Not only does this honor the Lord, but it also causes people who work with us to look at Christians more favorably. Christian employees and bosses should be the ones everyone wants as a coworker.

2.  A.  What task is given to us in Matthew 28:19–20?

    B.  Jesus tells us to be "witnesses." This means we evangelize best when we tell people about our own, personal encounter with the person of Jesus Christ. How has He touched you personally? How have you witnessed His unique and powerful love specifically for you?

"Modern man listens more willingly to witnesses than to teachers, and if he does listen to teachers, it is because they are witnesses." —Pope Paul VI

3. A. When Jesus asked us to step out in this way, did He expect it to be easy? See Matthew 10:16.

   B. What obstacles make it difficult for you to share about your faith at work or in public?

When Jesus sent His followers out as sheep in the midst of wolves, He was acknowledging that there would be persecution to follow. But what we consider to be persecution and a good excuse for not talking about our faith sounds pretty wimpy to Christians in the Middle East. I recently watched a documentary called *Sheep Among Wolves*.[104] It shares the story of Christians in Iran, a place where persecution is so intense that you would assume the Church would be dying. But the opposite is the case: it is exploding. In 2017, there were 350,000 Christians in Iran.[105] Today, that number is approaching one million.[106] The courage of those spreading the gospel is astounding.

One of the men interviewed in the documentary described going to an Iranian church service in a soundproofed room. When they walked into the meeting, everyone handed their cell phones to the guy at the door and the batteries were taken out. All the cell phones were dumped into a bathtub and covered with blankets and towels so nothing could be recorded and no one's location could be traced. Then everyone went into another room to quietly look at Scripture, pray, and worship. Everything was done in near-silence. They were whispering.

That's how they behaved privately, but speaking publicly about their faith is far riskier. Doing so causes many to be raped or killed, sometimes both. One particular conversation stands out to me, in which a woman explained to her husband that if she were raped because of her Christian faith, she wanted him to know that she considered it the living out of Romans 12:1, that she would be offering her body as a living sacrifice,

---

104 *Sheep Among Wolves, Volume I*, directed by Dalton Thomas (FAI Studios, February 2016), https://www.youtube.com/watch?v=Ndf8RqgNVEY.

105 Office of International Religious Freedom, "2017 Report on International Religious Freedom," U.S. Department of State, May 29, 2018, https://www.state.gov/reports/2017-report-on-international-religious-freedom/.

106 Jayson Casper, "Researchers Find Christians in Iran Approaching 1 Million," *Christianity Today*, September 3, 2020, https://www.christianitytoday.com/news/2020/september/iran-christian-conversions-gamaan-religion-survey.html.

holy and acceptable to God, as a form of worship. These believers are counting the cost, considering Jesus worth everything, and stepping out to witness.

    C.  Does this story cause you to look at your own obstacles any differently? What is the real consequence for us in sharing the gospel in the West? If you were to sit with an Iranian Christian to discuss those obstacles, what would you say?

4.  A.  When we feel that we are not up to the task of sharing our faith wherever we go, what comfort can we receive from 2 Corinthians 12:9?

    B.  When we feel that we aren't effective witnesses, what comfort can we receive from Saint Paul's words in 1 Corinthians 3:5–6?

"Every Christian is challenged, here and now, to be actively engaged in evangelization; indeed, anyone who has truly experienced God's saving love does not need much time or lengthy training to go out and proclaim that love. Every Christian is a missionary to the extent that he or she has encountered the love of God in Christ Jesus."[107] —Pope Francis

*Quiet your heart and enjoy His presence…He is with us in the noise and clatter of the office and the kitchen.*

*The patron saint of Walking with Purpose, Saint Thérèse of Lisieux, is also the patron saint of missions. It's interesting that Saint Thérèse never left the convent, yet Pope Paul XII said that she rediscovered the gospel for the modern world. Her "little way" increased our understanding of the importance of loving right where we are and, instead of feeling stressed and overwhelmed, trusting that in our weakness, God shows up and proves more than sufficient. She reminds us that we can be agents of change, right where we are. Whether our mission field is in one of the geographic areas of the world that are most hostile to the gospel, a school, an office, or the hiddenness of our homes, our witness matters.*

---

107  Pope Francis, *Joy of the Gospel* (Erlanger, KY: Dynamic Catholic Institute, 2014), 97.

*Dear Lord,*

*Whatever my task, may I "work heartily, as serving the Lord and not men." (Colossians 3:23)*

*May I "go and make disciples." (Matthew 28:19)*

*When I step out, may I be as wise as a serpent and innocent as a dove. (Matthew 10:16)*

*If I feel unqualified, may I remember that Your grace is sufficient for me, and Your power is made perfect in my weakness. (2 Corinthians 12:9)*

*May I never take credit for the results, nor hold back because of fear of failure, because You are the One who gives the growth. (1 Corinthians 3:5–6)*

*Amen.*

# Day Five
## YOU ARE AN AMBASSADOR FOR CHRIST

1.　A.　How is our role in society described in 2 Corinthians 5:20?




As ambassadors, we are serving in a foreign land as the representative of a king. Our mission isn't to speak in such a way that everyone around us likes us. The whole point is to deliver the message of the King who has sent us. But as ambassadors, we don't just deliver a message; we also represent the country we come from, the kingdom of God. We are to model a way of living that is evidence of the freedoms, privileges, and responsibilities of our homeland.

Father John Riccardo has taught me much about this subject through his Acts XXIX ministry. He asked me to think about the role of an embassy. An embassy is the headquarters of a government serving in a foreign country. It belongs to the country it represents and is not subject to the laws of the host country. It offers asylum and protection from arrest and extradition. If we are ambassadors for Christ, then the Church is the embassy. We are sent out from the embassy with an appeal, a message to carry to the foreign land where we live. And what is that message? *There is a safe haven.* In Father John's words, "You can defect. This is what we should be shouting. You don't have to live under the tyrant's regime."

　　B.　Do you see yourself as an ambassador for Christ? Do you see evidence of a tyrant's regime around you, a pressure to conform to a way of living that does not promote true flourishing?

2.   A.   Which two types of messengers are described in Proverbs 13:17, and what different results does each bring?

Our message is not one of condemnation; it's sharing a pathway to healing. People are continually bombarded with messages promising a better life, but not all those messages point to the path that leads to healing on the soul level. The message we share is one that leads to growth and fulfillment. It's good news, not bad.

   B.   Can you think of an example from your life of a time when the good news of the gospel brought healing to you?

3.   A.   In the midst of a pagan culture, how are Christians to be identified, according to John 13:34–35?

   B.   Do you think this is what makes Christians stand out today? Is that trait more noticeable in you than in most people? In other words, is our love radical? Why or why not?

In the words of C. S. Lewis, "Enemy-occupied territory—that is what this world is. Christianity is the story of how the rightful king has landed, you might say landed in disguise, and is calling us to take part in a great campaign of sabotage."[108] Our greatest tactic in this campaign is to love in such a way that people can find no other explanation than a supernatural force helping us to do the impossible.

   C.   Saint John of the Cross said, "In the evening of life, we will be judged on love alone." When you reflect on how you spend your day, is this the way you measure how well you spent your time?

---

[108] C. S. Lewis, *The C. S. Lewis Signature Classics* (New York: HarperCollins, 2017), 46.

4. A. Radical love seems good in theory, but we can quickly hit roadblocks that make it feel impossible. Forgiving the unforgivable, loving an enemy, serving the undeserving, and persevering when you want to quit are all things asked of a Christian. But how do we do it? What difference does Christ make according to Galatians 2:20?

B. Where do we find the power to love radically? See Acts 1:8 and CCC 733.

*Quiet your heart and enjoy His presence…May He fill us with what appeals to a watching, searching world.*

*In his encyclical* Joy of the Gospel, *Pope Francis wrote, "Christians have the duty to proclaim the Gospel without excluding anyone. Instead of seeming to impose new obligations, they should appear as people who wish to share their joy, who point to a horizon of beauty and who invite others to a delicious banquet. It is not by proselytizing that the Church grows, but 'by attraction.'"*[109]

*Dear Lord,*
*As Your ambassador, I want to represent You well to others. Help me to display Your joy so that it is clear that news about You is good. In the words of Tim Keller, You lead us to a "narrow spaciousness." It may seem limiting at the beginning, but when we enter into a relationship with You, we come into a beautiful spaciousness that cultivates vibrant, meaningful lives.*

*No matter where I am, help me to remember that You are continually making Your appeal to others through me. May my love be so radical that the only explanation for it would have to be Your divine power at work. May Christ live in me, may the Holy Spirit breathe in me, may the Father envelop me. I am Yours. Amen.*

## Conclusion

Can an ordinary person confront a giant with any hope of success? This was the question on everyone's mind when a young Israelite shepherd named David offered to square off against the strongest Philistine warrior, Goliath. The challenge David faced appeared insurmountable. Anyone analyzing the odds would have put their money on Goliath's victory. But David took down the giant with five stones and a slingshot.

---

109 Pope Francis, *Joy of the Gospel*, 18.

It all began with a challenge: Goliath himself. And perhaps that is where the end of this study finds you. You are looking at all these lessons, your resolutions, the gap between who you want to be and how things actually are. I wonder what your reality is—how you would describe your "Goliath."

Maybe for you that challenge is putting into practice the things that we've been discussing throughout this Bible study. You want to live your life intentionally, putting the most important things first in your life. But learning about it all and living it out are two different things.

Or maybe you have your priorities in order, but some of those priorities are people, and those people have needs that are the size of a mountain. You've done the work of making sure that you are the one who is supposed to be involved, and God's answer has been yes, it's you. You might be in an especially demanding period as a mother, daughter, or wife. You look at what is needed from you, and it's a challenge.

Or perhaps your obstacles are at work. What is expected of you is a lot. You are carrying a heavy load, and the deadlines just keep coming. You're trying to give everyone your best—those at work and the people who matter most to you. You're just trying to keep your head above water, but there's always one more thing that someone expects of you. This is a tremendous challenge.

And some of you are in ministry and can see how desperately so many people need Jesus. You are aware of the mental health crisis we face in the twenty-first century. You know so many people are without hope and purpose. You know that Christ can make all the difference. But doing ministry today isn't easy. It's hard to speak the truth about Christ into a culture that equates biblical truth and Catholic Church teaching with bigotry, narrow-mindedness, and hatred. You see the enormous need people have for Christ, but there are times you are afraid to speak up, and you feel paralyzed as to what you should do. This is a challenge.

Regardless of what the Goliath challenge is, we all tend to do something similar in response.

We measure what it's going to take to be successful. We scope out the problem. We become very aware of all that is working against us. That's what we see happening in 1 Samuel 17:4–7, when Goliath is sized up and analyzed. This passage records how tall he was, says that he had a helmet and armor that weighed about eighty pounds. He had shin guards of bronze, a javelin, and a heavy spear. It says in verse 24 that "all the men of Israel, when they saw the man, fled from him, and were much afraid." They took a look at the challenge and decided to accept defeat.

But I believe that you have got more grit than that. Yes, you've sized up your challenge, but you are still in the fight. You are still here. You care about experiencing victory in this area of your life. You've determined that you're going to do whatever it takes.

And this is what I think most of us do next.

We start looking around for the perfect stones. If it's going to be stones that take down Goliath, then we need to have just the right ones. And God watches, and shakes His head, and says, "The victory actually has nothing to do with the stones." It has everything to do with God infusing ordinary rocks with supernatural power. It's what *He* does that achieves the victory.

May we never forget this. Because if we do, we will be very prone to bitterness toward God. We'll start to look at Him and His expectations and determine that they are unrealistic and too heavy a burden. We'll wonder why God won't lower the bar so it's at a height that we can reach, when what He wants to do is lift us to greater heights because He is the one doing the heavy lifting.

As you endeavor to order your priorities, I pray you would also rest in the all-sufficiency of the Lord. He asks for your cooperation, but His is the power that makes all the difference.

*"Now therefore stand still and see this great thing, which the Lord will do before your eyes." (1 Samuel 12:16)*

# My Resolution

Examples:

1. I can recognize some areas of my life where I have failed to set boundaries with my extended family. I commit to not only setting those boundaries today but also sharing it with a friend, and asking her to hold me accountable.

2. I am longing for deeper, Christ-centered friendship. Instead of waiting for someone to reach out to me, I will initiate and invite _____ to get together one-on-one.

3. I recognize that my place of work is my mission field. I will not only take care to be a good witness of radical love in the workplace, I will also pray for this coworker, [his or her name], consistently.

My Resolution:

# Catechism Clips

*CCC 733* "God is Love" and love is his first gift, containing all others. "God's love has been poured into our hearts through the Holy Spirit who has been given to us."

# NOTES

# Lesson 8: Connect Coffee Talk 2

## TO THE HEIGHTS

Accompanying talk can be viewed via DVD or digital download purchase, or access online at walkingwithpurpose.com/videos.

*"Be amazed at the heights to which you are called."* —*Saint John Paul II*

I. **The Challenge to Ascend to the Heights**

Colossians 3:2


"It is Jesus who stirs in you the desire to do something great with your lives, the will to follow an ideal, the refusal to allow yourselves to be ground down by mediocrity, the courage to commit yourselves humbly and patiently to improving yourselves and society, making the world more human and more fraternal."[110] —Saint John Paul II

II. **The Mountains of Blessing and Curses**

Deuteronomy 27–28


Deuteronomy 30:11–20


III. **The Encounter That Changes Everything**

John 4:3–23

---

110 John Paul II, "15th World Youth Day."

Hosea 11:4–5, 8


Hosea 13:15


Hosea 14:4


Hosea 2:19–20


IV. **Leaving Your Water Jar**

Lisa's Nonnegotiables:

1. The second glass matters
2. I will be the guardian of Leo's reputation
3. Daily intercession for my children
4. Daily Bible reading
5. Creating home before work


"You aspire to great things? Begin with little ones." —Saint Augustine of Hippo


Psalm 121

# Discussion Questions:

1. When you read, "Choose life, that you and your descendants may live, loving the Lord your God, obeying his voice, and clinging to him" (Deuteronomy 30:19–20), does it bring to mind a decision or a choice you are currently facing or one from the past?

2. In the talk, Lisa said that "leaving her water jar behind" meant:

   *I put down what I feel like doing to pick up what I know to be life-giving.*

   *I put down what the world tells me is going to make me feel better to pick up what God says leads to true flourishing.*

   *I put down the to-do list and the tasks that scream for my attention to pick up restorative practices and habits that give my day the framework it needs.*

   What does this mean to you?

3. As you are challenged to ascend to the heights, what nonnegotiables might help you on that journey?

 NOTES

# NOTES

 NOTES

# NOTES

# NOTES

# NOTES

 NOTES

# Appendices

# NOTES

# Appendix 1
# Saint Thérèse of Lisieux

*Patron Saint of Walking with Purpose*

Saint Thérèse of Lisieux was gifted with the ability to take the riches of our Catholic faith and explain them in a way that a child could imitate. The wisdom she gleaned from Scripture ignited a love in her heart for her Lord that was personal and transforming. The simplicity of the faith that she laid out in her writings is so completely Catholic that Pope Pius XII said, "She rediscovered the Gospel itself, the very heart of the Gospel."

Walking with Purpose is intended to be a means by which women can honestly share their spiritual struggles and embark on a journey that is refreshing to the soul. It was never intended to facilitate the deepest of intellectual study of Scripture. Instead, the focus has been to help women know Christ: to know His heart, to know His tenderness, to know His mercy, and to know His love. Our logo is a little flower, and that has meaning. When a woman begins to open her heart to God, it's like the opening of a little flower. It can easily be bruised or crushed, and it must be treated with the greatest of care. Our desire is to speak to women's hearts no matter where they are in life, baggage and all, and gently introduce truths that can change their lives.

Saint Thérèse of Lisieux, the little flower, called her doctrine "the little way of spiritual childhood," and it is based on complete and unshakable confidence in God's love for us. She was not introducing new truths. She spent countless hours reading Scripture and she shared what she found, emphasizing the importance of truths that had already been divinely revealed. We can learn so much from her:

> The good God would not inspire unattainable desires; I can, then, in spite of my littleness, aspire to sanctity. For me to become greater is impossible; I must put up with myself just as I am with all my imperfections. But I wish to find the way to go to heaven by a very straight, short, completely new little way. We are in a century of inventions: now one does not even have to take the trouble to

climb the steps of a stairway; in the homes of the rich, an elevator replaces them nicely. I, too, would like to find an elevator to lift me up to Jesus, for I am too little to climb the rough stairway of perfection. So I have looked in the books of the saints for a sign of the elevator I long for, and I have read these words proceeding from the mouth of eternal Wisdom: "He that is a little one, let him turn to me" (Proverbs 9:16). So I came, knowing that I had found what I was seeking, and wanting to know, O my God, what You would do with the little one who would answer Your call, and this is what I found:

"As one whom the mother caresses, so will I comfort you. You shall be carried at the breasts and upon the knees they shall caress you" (Isaiah 66:12–13). Never have more tender words come to make my soul rejoice. The elevator which must raise me to the heavens is Your arms, O Jesus! For that I do not need to grow; on the contrary, I must necessarily remain small, become smaller and smaller. O my God, You have surpassed what I expected, and I want to sing Your mercies. (Saint Thérèse of the Infant Jesus, *Histoire d'une Ame: Manuscrits Autobiographiques* [Paris: Éditions du Seuil, 1998], 244.)

# Appendix 2
# The Divine Exchange

Some time ago, one of my children came home after months away. He was heartsick and devastated over decisions made and opportunities lost. As he poured out all that he had been carrying within, he said he felt like the prodigal son coming home with a bowed head and heavy heart. *My* heart, by contrast, was full of joy. The truth was, I wasn't shocked by anything he shared, and it all seemed worse to him than it was in reality. But that wasn't the source of my joy. It came from seeing that he had finally come to the end of himself, and as a result, he was looking up at God. I knew that angels in heaven were rejoicing along with me.

Typically, when we pray for ourselves and our loved ones, we ask God for health, a smooth road, job promotions, and all things pleasant. But what is often most needed (and the greatest gift from God) is for it all to come crashing down. When everything feels horrible and we realize that we cannot save ourselves, that we've dug ourselves into a hole and we are stuck, we are in the perfect position for deliverance to a truly abundant way of life.

Our pride really gets in the way of our experiencing the abundant life that Jesus promised us in John 10:10. As long as we believe we've got a couple of solutions up our sleeve, we remain blind to our desperate need for Jesus. Our starting point must be a recognition of our need.

I wonder, have you come to the end of yourself? Have you recognized your littleness before God? We think of the saints and their holiness, but the truth is, they started out in the same way you and I do. They were weak and in need of a savior. When they met Jesus, they never lost sight of who their rescuer really was, and that it was never, and never would be, themselves. This is seen clearly in the life of Saint Thérèse of Lisieux, who is known for her little way of spiritual childhood. She wrote:

> But I wish to find the way to go to Heaven by a very straight, short, completely new little way. We are in a century of inventions: now one does not even have to take the trouble to climb the steps of a stairway; in the homes of the rich an elevator replaces them nicely. I, too, would like to find an elevator to lift me up to Jesus, for I am too little to climb the rough stairway of perfection. So I have looked in the books of the saints for a sign of the elevator I long for, and I have read these words proceeding from the mouth of eternal Wisdom: "He that is a little one, let him turn to me."…The elevator which must raise me to the heavens

is Your arms, O Jesus! For that I do not need to grow; on the contrary, I must necessarily remain small, become smaller and smaller.[112]

Saint Thérèse realized at a very young age that self-reliance wasn't going to get her very far on the road to holiness. Fully recognizing her weaknesses and failures, she threw herself on the mercy of God. When she thought about what it would be like to stand before God at the end of her life, she reflected, "In the evening of my life I shall appear before You with empty hands, for I do not ask You to count my works. All our justices are stained in Your eyes. I want therefore to clothe myself in Your own justice and receive from Your love the eternal possession of Yourself."[113]

These thoughts come straight from Scripture. In Isaiah 64:6, we read, "All our just deeds are like polluted rags." If we come to God thinking that we are going to be accepted by Him based on our "good conduct," He will point out that our righteousness is nothing compared to His infinite holiness. God holds out a standard of holiness that is perfection—in action as well as in motive. According to Romans 6:23, "The wages of sin is death." Not just major sin. Any sin. This means that even a good deed performed with ill motive is enough to separate us from God for eternity. As Saint Thérèse said, "All our justices are stained in Your eyes."

If that were the end of the story, we would be facing a very dismal, hopeless future. But Romans 6:23 goes on to say, "But the free gift of God is eternal life in Christ Jesus our Lord." It is a free, undeserved gift of grace that God offers us. He knew that we would fail, and that something would need to fill the gap between our best efforts at holiness and His standard of perfection. His solution wasn't some*thing*. It was some*one*—His perfect, sinless son, Jesus.

Saint Thérèse recognized that her solution to her hopeless state was nothing other than the gospel. She said that if her justices or righteous deeds were stained, then she wanted to clothe herself in Christ's own justice. We see this described in 2 Corinthians 5:21: "For our sake, [God] made him to be sin who knew no sin, so that in him we might become the righteousness of God." This is the divine exchange—our sin for His righteousness.

How did God make Him who had no sin to be sin for us? This was foretold by the prophet Isaiah: "But he was pierced for our sins, crushed for our iniquities; he bore the punishment that makes us whole, by his wounds we were healed" (Isaiah 53:5). Jesus accomplished this on the cross. Now all His merits are ours. He fills our empty hands and hearts with His own virtues.

---

112  D'Elbee, *I Believe in Love*, 26–7.

113  Saint Thérèse's Act of Offering.

Yes, we are little. Yes, we are weak. Yes, we do fail, often. But God looks at our heart, and He sees our desire to trust Him, to please Him, to obey Him. And He will make up where we are lacking, if we ask Him.

God desires that we be like a child—confident in our Father. He is our heavenly Father, and when life feels like it's just too much, He wants us to crawl into His lap, holding all our cares and concerns, trusting that He is going to take care of everything. Because of Jesus, we can always hit the do-over button. He promises to restore the years that seem wasted to us. He can bring good from even the most horrible messes. He can repair what we have done badly and fill in the gaps when we leave things undone.

The divine exchange is on offer to each one of us. God's arms are extended to every person in the world; there is no sinner beyond the reach of His mercy. He invites us to give Him our sin, our regret, our garbage, our mistakes, our failures. His heart burns with such intense love for each one of us that all our mess goes into the divine incinerator of His heart and is no more. But He doesn't leave us empty. He takes our sin and then puts His very Spirit into our hearts. The Holy Spirit rushes in and fills us with divine love, joy, peace, patience, kindness, goodness, faithfulness, gentleness, and self-control.

God is a gentleman, and He won't force you to make this exchange. He waits for you. Have you come to the end of yourself? Are you ready to receive what He is offering you? If you are, you might consider praying this prayer:

Dear Lord,
I have come to the end of my best-laid plans and brightest ideas for fixing myself. The truth is, I can't do this on my own. I need a rescue. I know that if I were to come to You with a list of all the things that are pretty good about me, I would still fall short of what You ask of me, which is to be holy like Jesus. I'm not, Lord. Not even close.

So please break through all my pride, my self-reliance, and my excuses. I give You my heart, sinful as it is. I confess my sin to You and ask You to forgive me for each thing I have done, and for the fact that I have tried everything before finally surrendering to You.

And that's what I'm doing now. I am waving the white flag of surrender. I am lying prostrate before You, needy, sick, and broken. Please take all the garbage within me and burn it up in Your heart, which is a furnace of love. Save me.

I invite You into my heart. My heart is Your home. Come in and do all the cleaning and rearranging that is needed. I give myself to You. Please give Yourself to me. Amen.

 NOTES

# Appendix 3
# Who I Am in Christ

Do you wonder who you are? Do you struggle to define your worth by the right things? Read the following verses and rest in the truth that you are God's beloved daughter. You are worthy. You are accepted. You are loved.

## I Am God's Beloved Daughter and That Is Enough

*"In love, [God] destined us for adoption to himself through Jesus Christ"*
*(Ephesians 1:4–5).*

I am not an orphan. I am God's beloved daughter.

*"The one begotten by God he protects, and the evil one cannot touch him"*
*(1 John 5:18b).*

I am God's daughter. He protects me. The evil one cannot touch me.

*"For in [Jesus] dwells the whole fullness of the deity bodily, and you share in this fullness in him, who is the head of every principality and power" (Colossians 2:9–10).*

I am complete in Christ.

## I Am a New Creation

*"So whoever is in Christ is a new creation: the old things have passed away; behold, new things have come" (2 Corinthians 5:17).*

I am a new creature in Christ.

*"No longer I, but Christ lives in me; insofar as I now live in the flesh, I live by faith in the Son of God who has loved me and given himself up for me" (Galatians 2:20).*

Christ lives in me.

*"Put on the new self, which is being renewed, for knowledge, in the image of its creator"*
*(Colossians 3:10).*

I am done with my old life. My new self is being made in the image of my Creator.

## I Am Forgiven

*"In him we have redemption by his blood, the forgiveness of transgressions, in accord*
*with the riches of his grace that he lavished upon us" (Ephesians 1:7–8).*

I am forgiven for all my sins.

*"He himself bore our sins in his body upon the cross, so that, free from sin, we might*
*live for righteousness. By his wounds you have been healed" (1 Peter 2:24).*

I am healed by Christ's wounds.

*"If we acknowledge our sins, he is faithful and just and will forgive our sins and cleanse*
*us from every wrongdoing" (1 John 1:9).*

When I confess my sins, God forgives me, every time.

## I Am Free and Fully Alive

*"But God, who is rich in mercy, because of the great love he had for us, even when we*
*were dead in our transgressions, brought us to life with Christ (by grace you have been*
*saved)" (Ephesians 2:4–5).*

I am alive with Christ, saved by grace.

*"For the law of the spirit of life in Christ Jesus has freed you from the law of sin*
*and death" (Romans 8:2).*

I am free from the law of sin and death.

## *I Am Strong and Courageous*

*"In justice shall you be established, far from oppression, you shall not fear, from destruction, it cannot come near" (Isaiah 54:14).*

I am free from oppression, and fear will not master me.

*"The one who is in you is greater than the one who is in the world" (1 John 4:4).*

The One in me is greater than the evil one.

*"For God did not give us a spirit of cowardice but rather of power and love and self-control" (2 Timothy 1:7).*

God has not given me a spirit of fear, but one of power, love, and a sound mind.

*"In all circumstances, hold faith as a shield, to quench all the flaming arrows of the evil one" (Ephesians 6:16).*

I can quench all the fiery darts of the evil one with my shield of faith.

*"I can do all things through Christ who strengthens me" (Philippians 4:13).*

I can do all things through Christ.

*"In all these things we conquer overwhelmingly through him who loved us" (Romans 8:37).*

I am more than a conqueror through Him who loves me.

*"They conquered him by the blood of the Lamb and by the word of their testimony; love for life did not deter them from death" (Revelation 12:11).*

I am an overcomer by the blood of the Lamb and the word of my testimony.

## *I Am Filled with God's Peace*

*"We have the mind of Christ" (1 Corinthians 2:16).*

*"Have among yourselves the same attitude that is also yours in Christ Jesus" (Philippians 2:5).*

I have the mind of Christ.

*❦❦❦❦❦❦*

*"Then the peace of God that surpasses all understanding will guard your hearts and minds in Christ Jesus" (Philippians 4:7).*

I have the peace of God that surpasses all understanding.

# Appendix 4
# Great Spiritual Resources for Kids

## *Early Childhood*

## Music on Spotify:

*Big Stories for Little Ones* by Rain for Roots
*Come to the Cradle* by Michael Card
*The Donut Man*, Rob Evans (he has many different albums)
*Hide 'Em in Your Heart* by Steve Green
*Sleep Sound in Jesus* by Michael Card

## Books:

*Angel in the Waters* by Regina Doman
This hardback book tells a special story. It's the first story of every child of God: In its mother's womb, a tiny baby grows, explores the waters, and talks with the angel who is there.

*God Gave Us Heaven* by Lisa Tawn Bergren
This gentle story provides satisfying answers for a young child's most difficult questions about what happens after this life, inviting "little cubs" to find comfort in knowing that God gave us heaven.

*God Gave Us You* by Lisa Tawn Bergren
Perfect for bedtime, nap time, story time, or anytime, this book provides a valuable opportunity to build children's self-esteem every day and assure each one that he or she truly is a welcomed, precious, and treasured gift from above.

*Just in Case You Ever Wonder* by Max Lucado
I read this so many times, I have it memorized. So do my kids. This is a fabulous bedtime book (really anytime) and settles the heart beautifully. I can't recommend it enough.

*Lift the Flap Bible* by Sally Lloyd-Jones
This book of fourteen Bible stories keeps kids entertained with great illustrations, clear storytelling, and the fun of the flaps. It earns my two-year-old grandson's seal of approval.

***Light of Sunday*** by Geena Harrington and Katrina Harrington
This board book is a fabulous way to introduce your child to more than forty items associated with the Holy Mass. You can find this little treasure on sophiainstitute.com.

***Read Aloud Bible Stories (Volumes 1–4)*** by Ella K. Lindvall
I read these Bible stories so often to my children that the books have literally fallen apart.

***The Jesus Storybook Bible*** by Sally Lloyd-Jones
This children's Bible is an absolute gem because no matter the story being told, the author manages to make each one point to Jesus. It really impacted my kids' faith journey, and encouraged me along the way.

***Who Sang the First Song?*** by Ellie Holcomb
Ellie Holcomb also sings on the Rain for Roots album mentioned previously. The illustrations alone make this book fabulous, and the message about God singing creation into being is beautiful.

***The Word of the Lord: A Child's First Scripture Verses*** by Katie Warner
This board book introduces your child to core teachings and mysteries of the Catholic faith.

***You Are Special b***y Max Lucado
A must-have on your bookshelf—the perfect book when your child needs to know how special he or she is. There is great wisdom in this book that I referred back to all the way up into middle school in terms of who we allow to define our worth.

## *Elementary School*

## Music on Spotify:

(For the latest albums, search "kids praise and worship")

***Hillsong Kids***
***Bethel Music Kids***
***Elevation Church Kids***
***Orange Kids Music***
***Sing the Word from A to Z*** by the Harrow Family
    A great way to memorize Bible verses.
***Sing the Word: A New Commandment*** by the Harrow Family
    A great way to memorize Bible verses.

## Books:

***The Action Bible, illustrated*** by Sergio Cariello
The Action Bible presents more than 230 fast-paced narratives in chronological order, making it easy to follow the Bible's historical flow and building up to the thrilling climax of God's redemptive story.

***Can You Find Saints?*** by Philip D. Gallery
When I asked for recommendations, my eight-year-old daughter ran for this book and told me about everything she's learned from it.

***Catechism of the Seven Sacraments*** by Kevin O'Neill and Mary O'Neill
Set in a vivid comic-book format with stunning photographs, this Lego-inspired book makes profound theological concepts accessible to both the Catholic and the curious, the child and the adult.

***The Chronicles of Narnia*** by C. S. Lewis
Even without an understanding of the rich Christian symbolism in these books, the story is utterly captivating. But reading this fiction series aloud to your kids will help you all to catch glimpses of the ways in which taking your place in God's story is the best adventure of all.

***Daughter of the King*** by Terra Tucker
This is currently my absolute favorite to read to my youngest, and I cry every single time I read it. It's that good. It's also probably difficult to find because I bought it at a little shop in Franklin, Tennessee, called Imago Dei. But just in case you find a copy, I recommend it!

***The Garden, the Curtain, and the Cross*** by Carl Laferton
This excellent picture book illustrates what it took for God to be able to open the way to a relationship with Him. It's super clear and powerful—perfect for the younger elementary years.

***A Girl's Guide to Making Really Good Choices*** by Elizabeth George
This book addresses challenging topics like attitude, friendships, crushes, parents, and school to help girls ages eight to twelve let God, not the world, define who they are.

***GPS: God's Plan in Scripture*** by Ascension Press
This storybook connects the Bible with the Catholic faith, beginning in Genesis and ending in Revelation.

*Marian Consecration for Children: Bringing Mary to Life in Young Hearts and Minds* by Carrie Gress

This book provides a fun and thrilling way for children to participate in this centuries-old practice. In just a matter of weeks, they will come to know Mary as they never have before, allowing her to take their hand and lead them to Christ.

*NLT Girls Life Application Study Bible*

While this translation of the Bible is not Catholic, I found that the special feature called "Foundations for Your Faith" made all the difference for my daughter. She actually sits down and reads the Bible, by herself, without prompting. I added Bible tabs (pretty ones sold on Etsy).

*The End of the Fiery Sword: Adam & Eve and Jesus & Mary* by Maura Roan McKeegan

What do Adam and Jesus have in common? What do Eve and Mary have in common? More than you think! Discover similarities between persons or events in the Old Testament that foreshadow those of the New Testament.

*Starting Strong* by Paula Rinehart

This is a consumable book that helps preteens learn how to study the Bible on their own. It includes stories, stickers, questions, and activities.

*St. Mother Teresa of Calcutta Story Card Set* by the CFR Franciscans and Greenhouse Collective

This beautiful set of cards, when placed together, makes a large puzzle-like illustration of the life of Saint Teresa of Calcutta. Each flash card piece features an event in her life, and the reverse side tells a story and includes questions, Scripture, and an activity to help kids learn to follow Jesus. There is a set for Saint Thérèse of Lisieux, Saint John Paul II, and Saint Francis of Assisi as well. Available for purchase from the Abiding Together podcast website under "shop" (abidingtogetherpodcast.com).

*Take It to the Queen* by Josephine Nobisso

With exquisite artwork and evocative text, this original fable explores the events of Jesus' life, and demonstrates the role of the Virgin Mary as the benevolent agent of God's people.

*The Weight of a Mass* by Josephine Nobisso and Katalin Szegedi

In this original fairy tale based on a true event, a miracle converts the hearts of a once-cold kingdom when a widow begs stale bread in return for offering her participation in the royal wedding Mass.

*The Wingfeather Saga* by Andrew Peterson

This fiction series helps kids to long to be a part of the epic tale God is writing. It's a great follow-up to *The Chronicles of Narnia*.

## *Middle School*

### BLAZE resources

BLAZE is Walking with Purpose's middle school girls' ministry. We offer two years of curriculum (***Masterpiece*** and ***Belong***) along with a fun kit full of take-home gifts that make the lessons entertaining and meaningful. We also have a Bible Study called ***Discovering My Purpose*** and a mother-daughter devotional called ***Between You and Me***. All these resources address identity, body image, friendship, and spiritual growth by looking at the lies of our culture and comparing them with the truths of Scripture.

### Axis.org

I know of no better resource at the moment for this age group (and beyond) than Axis. Their mission is to connect parents, teens, and Jesus in a disconnected world, and give parents and mentors hope by being a guide through culture into conversation around Jesus. Their newsletter (Culture Translator) and their parent-child conversation guides are cutting-edge and immensely practical. Things are changing at breakneck speed and most of us aren't sure how to delve into current topics like gender, sexuality, porn, racism, and anxiety. The Culture Translator is free, and the conversation guides are available through a membership program. Don't shy away from this—it's worth every penny.

### Camps:

**Edge Summer Camp through Life Teen in Tiger, GA**
*https://lifeteen.com/camps/camp-hidden-lake/*

**Camp Wojtyla in Erie, CO**
*http://www.camp-w.com*

## *High School*

### Books:

***A Second Look: Encountering the True Jesus* by Mark Hart**
This book explores twelve stories of Jesus and brings teens into an encounter with Him.

***Blessed Are the Bored in Spirit*** by Mark Hart
This is a personal recommendation from my oldest daughter; it was a real favorite of hers.

***The Case for a Creator*** by Lee Strobel
This is a fabulous book for someone who struggles to believe that God exists. It makes the case for a Creator through science and is a fascinating read.

***Catholic Teen Bible*** by Life Teen
I cannot count how many of these Bibles I have purchased and given as gifts. It's the Bible all my kids used throughout high school and college.

***Chasing Humility*** by Joel Stepanek
This book covers eight ways to shape a Christian heart.

***Come Adore*** by Life Teen
A pocket-size guide to Adoration.

***Come Clean*** by Life Teen
A pocket-size guide to the sacrament of Reconciliation.

***Come Pray*** by Life Teen
A pocket-size guide to prayer.

***Come Walk*** by Life Teen
A pocket-size guide to the journey of spiritual transformation.

***Heart of an Athlete*** by the Fellowship of Christian Athletes
This book has 120 short reflections aimed at athletes. It goes straight to the issues that matter most, such as identity, fear, trust, and recognition.

***I Choose the Sky*** by Emily Wilson
A scriptural devotional by one of the most popular Catholic speakers among young adults.

***Rekindled: How Jesus Called Me Back to the Catholic Church and Set Me on Fire*** by Mallory Smyth
Mallory articulates well the frustration that leads many young people to walk away from the faith, and then gives practical guidance for keeping it or reengaging even when what you encounter in the Church falls short. My daughter found this book to be both relatable and very helpful.

## Walking with Purpose young adult Bible studies

Our six young adult Bible studies are adapted from two of our highly rated adult women studies, *Opening Your Heart* and *Keeping in Balance*. Each study is six weeks long, and perfect for young adults to do on their own or in a small group. Immensely practical, they are great tools for learning how to study the Bible and making it a daily habit.

Be sure to take a look at the Life Teen shop for many more resources in addition to the ones I mention here (shop.lifeteen.com).

## Camps and Conferences:

### Life Teen Camp Covecrest in Tiger, GA
*https://lifeteen.com/camps/camp-covecrest/*
All my kids have gone to Covecrest and found it to be truly transformational.

### Life Teen Camp Hidden Lake in Dahlonega, GA
*https://lifeteen.com/camps/camp-hidden-lake/*

### Life Teen Camp Wild Sky in Medina, TX
*https://lifeteen.com/camps/camp-wild-sky/*

### Camp Wojtyla in Erie, CO
*http://www.camp-w.com*

### Catholic Youth Summer Camp (CYSC) at Damascus Catholic Mission campus in Centerburg, Ohio
*https://cysc.com*
My daughter went to Camp Damascus and experienced amazing spiritual growth and community. The summer missionaries are incredibly well trained.

### Steubenville Youth Conferences
*https://steubenvilleconferences.com/youth/*

### Life Teen Leadership Conference at Benedictine College in Atchinson, KS
*https://lifeteen.com/events/life-teen-leadership-conference/*
This conference was the single best thing I ever sent my children to. Every time, it required sacrifice, preplanning, and organization to make it happen. And each time, the experience transformed my kids in profound, unique ways.

# Appendix 5
# Connecting with the Spiritually Indifferent

I'd like to share four steps we can take to help the spiritually indifferent and those who are searching for spiritual beliefs that really matter.

**Step 1: Ask good questions and really listen to the answers.**

Asking good questions offers a young person a safe place to process and wrestle with ideas. I encourage you to resist the urge to jump in quickly with your own answer. I'm not saying to *never* share how you answer these questions. But wait until they ask for your thoughts. It may be years of waiting, but better to speak your truth when someone is actually listening to what you have to say.

After you pitch the question, actively listen, then thank the person for being willing to share honestly. And if it's true, let him or her know that you learned something because of what was shared.

Here are some examples of meaty questions that can help your loved one to think about the deeper things of life:

- How would you answer the question "Who am I?"
- Fast-forward five years. What qualities would you want to be true of you?
- Why do you think you are here?
- What do you think is the best way to find real love?
- What does it mean to you to be happy and live a good life?
- What do you think are some good ways to focus on what matters and live up to your truest potential?
- How do you think you can experience lasting peace?
- How do you choose friends? How can you discern the difference between a toxic friendship and a healthy one?
- Do you ever find yourself doing things you know you shouldn't (and on some level don't want to do), but feel that you just can't help it?
- If a friend came to you and told you that she felt she was changing (and not in a good way), how would you advise her to go back to a better version of herself?

**Step 2: Point out that *any* belief system will involve a leap of faith—even one rooted in science and reason.**

Our culture gives great credence to that which can be proven by data and statistics. This makes sense. But we make a huge mistake when we assume that science is that which can be proven, while faith is something less tangible and therefore unreliable.

Listen to the words of atheist biologist Richard Lewontin:

> Our willingness to accept scientific claims that are against common sense is the key to an understanding of the real struggle between science and the supernatural. *We take the side of science in spite of the patent absurdity of some of its constructs,* in spite of its failure to fulfill many of its extravagant promises of health and life, in spite of the tolerance of the scientific community for unsubstantiated just-so-stories, *because we have a prior commitment,* a commitment to materialism.[114]

Author J. R. R. Tolkien believed that myths can convey foundational truth. This is what lies behind his writing, what makes it truly powerful. It's a literary technique that C. S. Lewis also used, and the two of them often discussed how to do this in the most effective way. We hear the word *myth* and we think, *Oh, that's something that's not true.* But myth is actually a method of explaining things that are difficult to put into a theorem. Why is it used? Because we learn best through story. We grasp stories, we relate to them, and as a result, we remember them better.

While Tolkien believed that myths can convey foundational truth, he also believed that we have been duped into using the word *myth* as synonymous with a lie, that we've been duped into accepting the first real lie of the philosophy of materialism—the claim that there is no supernatural order to the universe. Materialists believe that what we see is all that exists. In convincing us of this, they have actually imprisoned us in a world of mere matter.

Tolkien believed that the materialists were lying—that they were the ones with a false myth. That *their* world is the one that doesn't exist—that it was, in fact, a figment of their imagination. But, he observed, the problem is that they have convinced us. They have made us believe that this is all there is! Three dimensions, five senses, four walls, when there is so much more.

---

114 Richard C. Lewontin, "Billions and Billions of Demons," *The New York Review,* January 9, 1997, https://www.nybooks.com/articles/1997/01/09/billions-and-billions-of-demons/.

Many scientists have a bias toward materialism, and this bias helps them to take a leap of faith in accepting some scientific claims.

Any belief system will involve a leap of faith, even one rooted in science and reason. Even believing in the philosophy of materialism requires a leap of faith. One could question whether what is seen, what is material, is really there, or whether we are living in the Matrix—a state of virtual reality. Materialists take a leap of faith and say, "No, I do not believe we are living in a state of virtual reality," but they cannot prove it. They cannot prove that we are not all just hallucinating.

People take a leap of faith in embracing atheism and then read and open their minds to things that confirm that way of thinking, and in doing so, they cement that view. We do the same with Christianity, certainly.

But take a look at each belief system and run with it to its logical conclusion. Where does moral relativism leave you? Where does atheism leave you? In a purposeless existence. In despair.

How can someone content themselves with such a meaningless conclusion? Is it not fair to ask which belief system has an end result that we actually want? Why would anyone want to end up in a place of confusion and despair? I understand the fear of being made to look the fool. No one likes to be lied to. Nobody wants to be deluded. We spot hypocrites. We hate fake. We don't want to be on the receiving end of deception. But if there is a leap of faith either way, wouldn't you prefer that the one ending with the fulfillment of your desires and a life of purpose is the one that is true?

And if it might be true, wouldn't it be worth exploring?

Which brings us to the next step…

### Step 3: Challenge our kids re: how much they have *truly* explored Christianity.

Does your child think he or she has explored Christianity already? If the answer is yes, Blaise Pascal might disagree. Read what he wrote centuries ago:

> Man despises religion. They hate it, and fear it is true…They think they have made great effort to learn when they have spent a few hours reading some books of the Bible, and have questioned some ecclesiastic about the truths of the faith. After that they boast that they have sought without success in books and among men.[115]

---

115  Blaise Pascal, *Pensées,* trans. A. J. Krailsheimer (New York: Penguin Classics, 1995), 4, 127–8.

According to Pascal, a true search requires some time and serious digging.

When N. T. Wright was the chaplain of the University of Oxford, he tried to meet with each new student. Many would say something like, "You won't be seeing much of me—I don't believe in God." Wright would ask them which god they don't believe in. They'd describe the god they don't believe in, and Wright would say, "Oh. I don't believe in that god either. I believe in the God who was revealed in Jesus of Nazareth."[116]

These thoughts are echoed by Archbishop Fulton Sheen:

> There are not over a hundred people in the United States who hate the Catholic Church. There are millions, however, who hate what they wrongly believe to be the Catholic Church—which is, of course, quite a different thing.
>
> Our great country is filled with what might be called marginal Christians, i.e., those who live on the fringe of religion and who are descendants of Christian living parents, but who now are Christians only in name…They are good people who want to do the right thing, but who have no definite philosophy concerning it. They educate their children without religion, and yet they resent the compromising morals of their children. They would be angry if you told them they were not Christian, and yet they do not believe that Christ is God. They resent being called pagans and yet they never take a practical cognizance of the existence of God.
>
> There is only one thing of which they are certain and that is that things are not right as they are. It is just that single certitude which makes them what might be called the great "potentials," for they are ready to be pulled in either of two directions. Within a short time they must take sides; they must either gather with Christ or they must scatter; they must either be with Him or against Him; they must either be on the cross as other Christs, or under it as other executioners. Which way will these marginal Christians tend?…Only this much is certain. Being human and having hearts they want more than class struggle and economics; they want Life, they want Truth, and they want Love. In a word, they want Christ.[117]

---

116 Matt Nelson, *Just Whatever: How to Help the Spiritually Indifferent Find Beliefs That Really Matter* (El Cajon, CA: Catholic Answers, 2018), 64.

117 Tod Worner, "Father Fulton Sheen and the Millions Who Hate the Catholic Church," June 20, 2016, https://aleteia.org/2016/06/20/father-fulton-sheen-the-millions-who-hate-the-catholic-church/.

They want life, they want truth, they want love, they want Christ. If this is true, then we are obligated to take Step 4.

**Step 4: Give them a vision for what life *could be*.**

Here's a compelling question:

What if there's more?

When asked how to evangelize in a culture that is indifferent to God and religion, Bishop Robert Barron said that we should begin with the beautiful, which leads you to the good, which points you to the truth. We need to show that Christianity is attractive. As Blaise Pascal famously said, we are to make good men wish it was true.

So how do we do this? How do we begin with the beautiful? One way is to increase our exposure to beautiful and good literature, art, and music. The imagination can offer a spiritual opening as we begin to consider the possibility that there is something of meaning, something that moves us, something more than the superficial things that surround us.

This is an enormous opportunity, because this is not what our culture is offering people. Great literature? Great theater? Great art? This is something most of us haven't been exposed to, and moving in this direction won't cause an immediate shutdown because we haven't used the name of God or Jesus. It's coming in through the back door.

Look for the hook. As you talk to a spiritually indifferent person, search for what he is interested in. In what way is your loved one seeking beauty, goodness, or truth? That's your hook, the string you need to grab hold of and follow. Point out the goodness of that pursuit, and tell him that this is evidence that God is calling to him, summoning him to something greater.

Perhaps there is someone in your life who is spiritually searching, but she is searching in the wrong direction. You are probably really tempted to point out what is wrong about her search. I would encourage you to resist that temptation.

You might want to consider writing a letter instead and pointing out the things she is doing *well*. Is she seeking truth? Desiring a life of purpose? Let her know you are proud of her. This is something we never stop needing to hear.

What might a letter like this sound like? I offer this one as an example—not as the perfect one, just my humble attempt:

*Dear Joe, (not this person's real name)*

*I have always admired the way that you search for truth and excellence. You are willing to do the hard things required and have displayed a teachable spirit that is hungry to grow, to improve, to excel. You want your life to matter. You have a passion for living—a passion to know, to do and be all that is possible. This makes you unusual and poised to make a difference in our world.*

*You stand at the threshold of adulthood. When most people are distracting themselves and just having fun, you are paying attention and thinking deeply. I don't claim to know what your deep thoughts are, but I do see that you are wrestling. You are digging. You are looking for answers. To that I have to say, well done. Most people wait to ask the big questions until they are much older, and later feel they have wasted much of their lives. I don't think that will be said about you.*

*I know you want to live a life of meaning and purpose. I know of no better way to do that than to experiment and check out the different philosophies of life. We can consider the different ways of looking at life's meaning and compare them. Try them out. Discover which one actually works. And by works, I mean makes you happy.*

*Isn't that where everyone wants to end up? We all want to be happy. And to figure out what will make us happy requires our head and our heart. One of the things the heart helps us to figure out is what is real happiness. If something isn't going to satisfy your heart's longings deep down, either now or in the future, then your heart knows to look elsewhere. You've seen that happen in dating relationships. This isn't something that was proven by the scientific method; your heart just knew.*

*As you search for answers and meaning, it will always be tempting to turn to data and science to prove or disprove the various ways of looking at life and answering its biggest questions. I would encourage you to engage your head and to learn all you can, but not to rule out truths that are unseen. This is especially critical if you are trying to figure out if God exists. Would Hamlet have thought Shakespeare existed? Shakespeare couldn't be perceived or seen by him. But he was certainly there all along, writing the grand narrative.*

*I have a challenge for you. I encourage you to write down three things that you have to accomplish in your life. Three things that if you don't do them, you will feel you are a failure. Imagine being on your deathbed. Which choices do you wish you would have made?*

*The world is screaming at you that the goals you should be pursuing are:*
*Lots of sex*
*Lots of money and possessions*
*Lots of pleasure*

*Yet when people are asked at the end of their lives what their greatest regrets are, the majority say things like this:*

*I wish I had spent more time with my kids.*
*I wish I had a relationship with God.*
*I wish I had told people I loved them.*

*Most people don't think their goals through to the end. You know that. Many people are telling you that now is the time to just have fun. You are too smart to fall for that. You are investing in your future.*

*Pursue truth and love and you will not go wrong.*
*The good life is not about productivity—that never ultimately satisfies.*

*Praying that you find the program of living that brings you the deepest fulfillment,*
*Lisa*

What did I not say?

I did not say, "You are barking up the wrong tree and you are making me nervous, scared, and upset."

I did not say, "These are all the things you are doing wrong and they are going to leave you deeply unhappy."

I did not lay out the various philosophies that all say they have the secret to life's meaning. I want him to come back and ask me about that if he so desires. I am trying to stir up curiosity, not give answers to questions that aren't necessarily being asked.

I did not tell him which goals he should have. He needs to wrestle through this. When someone hands us something like this, we often don't own it, we just nod our heads and agree that it's true. But it doesn't transform us. Discovering things for ourselves (often the hard way) is a more effective teacher.

But asking, "What if there's more?" and then exposing them to the good, true, and beautiful can be a great way to begin giving loved ones a taste of what life with Christ could be.

There is so much more to say about all this. And I pray that you start having more conversations with your loved ones about the topics of meaning in life, purpose, what we want out of life, how we can be truly fulfilled, and how we can be happy. I encourage you to enter into these conversations and listen. To resist the urge to give the answer. To allow your children the space to wrestle and process without tying it up with a neat bow at the end. The truth is, life is messy and the journey of faith is full of detours and roadblocks. While you can play a part in smoothing the road, it will never be obstacle-free. But be patient. God is at work.

# Appendix 6
# Morning and Evening Routines

## *Morning Routine*

- Get up at 6 a.m.
- Make bed
- Shower
- Get dressed
- Do makeup and hair
- Put in load of laundry (goal is four loads by 4 p.m.)
- Make tea or coffee
- Prayer and Bible reading time
- Check calendar
- Make and eat breakfast
- Take vitamins
- Drive kids to school
- Check email
- Make phone calls
- Twenty-item pickup (pick up 20 items that are not in the right place and put them away)
- Thaw anything needed for dinner

## *Evening Routine*

- Look over calendar for tomorrow
- Charge phone/laptop
- Evening snack dishes in dishwasher
- Set tray with items for morning tea
- Fill kettle with water
- Pick up TV room
- Make sure kitchen is clean
- Put clothes away and lay out clothes for tomorrow
- Brush and floss teeth
- Wash and moisturize face
- Kiss kids good night
- Examination of conscience and nightly prayers
- In bed by 10 p.m.
- Read novel for fifteen minutes

 NOTES

# Answer Key

## Lesson 2, Day One

1. God is love. He showed His love for us by sending His only begotten Son into the world. "God shows His love for us in that while we were yet sinners Christ died for us" (Romans 5:8). No one has ever seen God, but Jesus, the only begotten Son, has made Him known. If we want to understand who God is, we need to look at Jesus.

2. God made Jesus to be sin who knew no sin, so that in Him we might become the righteousness of God.

3. **Psalm 68:5–6** God is the father of the fatherless and gives the desolate a home to dwell in.

   **Psalm 91:1–4** God shelters you. He is your refuge and fortress. He delivers you and covers you, offering you refuge under His wings. His faithfulness to you acts as a shield.

   **Jeremiah 31:3** God has loved you with an everlasting love.

   **Revelation 3:20** God stands at the door of your heart and knocks.

4. **Song of Solomon 1:15–16** God sees us as beautiful, truly lovely, His beloved.

   **Song of Solomon 2:4** God brings us into His banqueting house and puts a banner of love over us.

   **Song of Solomon 8:6–7** God's love for us is stronger than death. Peter Kreeft explains what this means in his book, *Three Philosophies of Life*: "At the point of death, a great battle is waged for the heavy-weight championship of the universe: in this corner Death, and in that corner Love. But death cannot change love; love changes death. Love changes the meaning of death, but death does not change the meaning of love. When fire and water meet, one must die. 'Love is strong as death' (Song 8:6) because 'many waters cannot quench love, neither can flood drown it' (Son 8:7)."[111]

## Lesson 2, Day Two

1. **A.** God's "sheep" hear His voice. God knows His sheep, and they follow Him.

   **B.** There are those who will try to climb into the sheep pen instead of going through the gate. They are thieves and robbers. But the true shepherd comes through the gate. The sheep hear His voice calling them by name. He leads them out, and they follow Him, because they know His voice. They won't follow a stranger because they don't know the voice of the stranger.

   **C.** "Fear not, for I have redeemed you; I have called you by name, you are mine. When you pass through the waters, I will be with you; and through the rivers, they shall not overwhelm you; when you walk through fire you shall not be burned, and the flame shall not consume you." (Isaiah 43:1–2)

---

111 Kreeft, *Three Philosophies of Life*, 139.

2. **A.** Some examples of voices in our heads: our thoughts, a parent's voice, a teacher's voice, a boss's voice, a high school bully's voice, a husband's voice, the enemy's voice.

   **B.** God's thoughts aren't like ours. They are higher than our own.

3. **A.** God sent Jesus into the world to save it, not to condemn it.

   **B.** Scripture is useful for teaching, reproof, correction, and training in righteousness.

4. **A.** We have to be still and know that He is God.

   **B.** Answers will vary.

## Lesson 2, Day Three

1. **A.** Our enemy is a murderer and has nothing to do with the truth. There is no truth in him. He is a liar and the father of lies. He is called the deceiver of the whole world.

   **B.** He disguises himself as an angel of light.

   **C.** "Behind the disobedient choice of our first parents lurks a seductive voice, opposed to God, which makes them fall into death out of envy. Scripture and the Church's Tradition see in this being a fallen angel, called 'Satan' or the 'devil.' The Church teaches that Satan was at first a good angel, made by God: 'The devil and the other demons were indeed created naturally good by God, but they became evil by their own doing.'" (CCC 391)

   Our enemy is an actual being. His voice is opposed to God. He is a fallen angel. He was made by God, was a good angel at first, but later became evil by his own doing. It's important to note that our enemy is not on equal standing with God. Our enemy is a creature, and God supersedes him in power.

   **D.** Jesus said that the ruler of this world was going to be cast out.

2. We are to destroy arguments and every proud obstacle to the knowledge of God, and take every thought captive to Christ.

3. Answers will vary.

4. **Deuteronomy 31:6** God is with you. He will never fail you or forsake you.

   **Psalm 46:1** God is your refuge and strength. He is a very present help in trouble.

   **Psalm 139:1** God knows you.

   **Jeremiah 29:11** God knows your future.

   **Jeremiah 32:17** Nothing is too hard for God.

   **Lamentations 3:22–23** God's steadfast love never ceases and His mercies are new every morning. Great is His faithfulness.

   **Malachi 3:6** God will never change.

   **Luke 1:37** Nothing is impossible for God.

**1 Corinthians 10:13** God is faithful, and He won't let you be tempted beyond your strength. When temptation comes, He will provide a way out, a way of escape.
**Ephesians 2:4** God is rich in mercy and loves us with a great love.
**1 John 1:9** God always forgives you when you ask.

## Lesson 2, Day Four

1.  Answers will vary.
2.  **A.** In the morning, before the sun rose, Jesus went out to a lonely place and prayed.
    **B.** They were to prepare the way of the Lord by making straight paths, filling valleys, bringing mountains and hills low, making the crooked straight, and the rough ways smooth.
    **C.** Answers will vary.
3.  **A.** **Matthew 6:31–33** We'll always be tempted to worry about the things we want and need, but Jesus tells us to seek God's kingdom first. If we do, He promises that God will give us all we need.
    **Colossians 1:15–18** Everything in the world (us included) was created through Jesus and for Jesus. He holds everything and everyone together. He is the head of the body (the Church). He is the beginning. He is to be preeminent in everything.
    **B.** Answers will vary.
4.  "Do not be conformed to this world but be transformed by the renewal of your mind, that you may prove what is the will of God, what is good and acceptable and perfect." (Romans 12:2)

## Lesson 2, Day Five

1.  **A.** Apart from Christ we can do nothing.
    **B.** Jesus warns His disciples that if they do not abide in Him, they'll be cast out, will wither, and will be burned.
2.  If we abide in Christ, four things will happen: 1) Our prayers will be answered. 2) We'll bear much fruit. 3) God will be glorified. 4) It will prove that we are Christ's disciples.
3.  **A.** We abide in Christ's love by obeying His commandments.
    **B.** Answers will vary.
    **C.** "From the beginning, Jesus associated his disciples with his own life, revealed the mystery of the Kingdom to them, and gave them a share in his mission, joy, and sufferings. Jesus spoke of a still more intimate communion between him and those who would follow him: 'Abide in me, and I in you... I am the vine,

you are the branches.' And he proclaimed a mysterious and real communion between his own body and ours: 'He who eats my flesh and drinks my blood abides in me, and I in him.'" (CCC 787)

This passage of the Catechism describes the mysterious, real, and intimate communion between Jesus' body and ours as what happens when we receive Him in the Eucharist. As it says in John 5:56, "He who eats my flesh and drinks my blood abides in me, and I in him."

4. Answers will vary.

## Lesson 3, Day One

1. Answers will vary.
2. **Matthew 9:4** When we think of the heart, we often think of our emotions. But this verse makes clear that our thoughts (usually associated with our minds) have something to do with our hearts.

   **John 16:22** Our hearts contain joy. As you would likely expect, our hearts contain our emotions.

   **Acts 11:23** (NABRE version) This verse talks about remaining faithful to the Lord in firmness of heart. It is speaking of using our will, determining to do something—namely, to remain faithful. So the will is a part of the heart.

   **Hebrews 10:22** We draw near to God with our hearts. Our hearts are sprinkled clean from an evil conscience in the waters of baptism. Our consciences are a part of our hearts.
3. Hidden center, Spirit of God, decision, encounter, relation
4. "The heart is deceitful above all things, and desperately corrupt; who can understand it?" (Jeremiah 17:9)
5. Psalm 51:6 teaches that God desires that truth dwell in our inner being. The psalmist asks God to teach him wisdom in his secret heart.

   *Personalized Prayer:* Dear God, I know that you desire that truth reign in my heart instead of lies. So please teach me wisdom in my secret heart. I don't even see all the places where I need your wisdom to replace my faulty thinking, but You do. Holy Spirit, You can fathom the human heart, but not just in a general sense. You know my heart fully. Please go into my hidden center and teach me. Amen.

## Lesson 3, Day Two

1. Answers will vary.
2. **A. Psalm 103:12** You are forgiven. God has thrown your sin as far as the east is from the west.

**Isaiah 43:1** God has called you by name. You belong to Him.

**John 15:16** You are chosen.

**1 Corinthians 8:3** You are known by God.

**Ephesians 1:4–6** You are not an orphan. You are God's beloved daughter.

B. Answers will vary.

3. A. "The dignity of the human person is rooted in his creation in the image and likeness of God (article 1); it is fulfilled in his vocation to divine beatitude (article 2). It is essential to a human being freely to direct himself to this fulfillment (article 3)" (CCC 1700). This means that we have inherent dignity because we are created in the image and likeness of God.

B. "The sinner wounds God's honor and love, his own human dignity as a man called to be a son of God, and the spiritual well-being of the Church, of which each Christian ought to be a living stone." (CCC 1487)

We wound our dignity when we sin. Sinning does not remove our dignity, but it violates it.

4. A. Jesus said that whoever wants to save his life needs to lose it, but whoever loses his life for Christ's sake will find it.

B. Answers will vary.

## Lesson 3, Day Three

1. A. Answers will vary.

B. Answers will vary.

C. Answers will vary.

2. A. For everything there is a season. We aren't meant to do everything all at once.

B. Answers will vary.

3. A. These verses are speaking about what we put in front of our eyes. We're told to not put anything that is base (worthless or wicked) before our eyes, and to turn our eyes away from vanities (worldly, meaningless things that distract).

B. We're told to look carefully how we walk, not as unwise people but as wise people. We do this by making the most of our time.

C. Answers will vary.

4. A. We are to remember the Sabbath day and keep it holy. We are to rest on the seventh day. On the Sabbath day we are not to work; we are to rest.

B. Answers will vary.

C. Answers will vary.

## Lesson 3, Day Four

1. You were made in the image and likeness of God.
2. **A.** My body is a temple of the Holy Spirit. I am to glorify God in my body.
   **B.** No, my body is not my own. It was bought at a price—not with silver or gold, "but with the precious blood of Christ" (1 Peter 1:19).
3. **A.** Rising early and going to bed late to anxiously achieve more is not the way God wants us to live. God grants His beloved sleep.
   Answers will vary.
   **B.** We are to think about things that are true, honorable, just, pure, lovely, gracious, excellent, and worthy of praise.
   Answers will vary.
   **C.** We are to exercise self-control in all things. We aren't running aimlessly. In fact, we were "created in Christ Jesus for good works, which God prepared beforehand, that we should walk in them" (Ephesians 2:10). But this life is a marathon, not a sprint. We want to run the race of our lives in such a way that we can reach the finish line.
   Answers will vary.
   **D.** Instead of filling our bodies with alcohol, we are to be filled with the Holy Spirit. We are given the gift of the indwelling Holy Spirit in the sacraments of Baptism and Confirmation. But we can ask for an increase of the Spirit's power to be released in us.
   Answers will vary.
4. Answers will vary.

## Lesson 3, Day Five

1. Our thinking should be mature. The opposite of maturity is being a child in your thinking.
2. "Age of body does not determine age of soul" (CCC 1308). Maturity doesn't automatically happen just because we are getting older and have more life experience. The key teaching point being made here is that although Confirmation is called the sacrament of Christian maturity, spiritual maturity can come earlier. A child, having received the Holy Spirit, can show remarkable Christian maturity. The reverse is also true. An adult who has received all the sacraments and lived many decades can choose to not cooperate with the grace being given and continue to think in a childish way.
3. A mature Christian is described as a person who is filled with the knowledge of God's will. She has spiritual wisdom and understanding, and uses what she knows

to "lead a life worthy of the Lord, fully pleasing to him, bearing fruit in every good work and increasing in the knowledge of God" (Colossians 1:10).

4. Answers will vary.

## Lesson 4, Day One

1. **A.** Marriage is described as the man leaving his father and mother and clinging to his wife. The two of them then become one flesh.

   **B.** In many marriages, one or both spouses fail to switch their loyalty over from their family of origin to the new family. Examples abound of in-laws having an unhealthy level of influence over a couple. Setting boundaries is not easy, but it is essential for a healthy marriage. Another way we can fall short is in failing to become one flesh. Affairs or withholding sex as a punishment both get in the way of "one flesh" intimacy.

2. God is described as an "eternal exchange of love" between the Father, Son and Holy Spirit. God has destined us to share in that exchange of love.

3. **A.** We so often do the opposite of what we know we should do. We don't do what we want (which would be loving well and sacrificially) and instead do the very things we hate (behaving selfishly).

   **B.** Answers will vary.

4. Jesus said that what God has joined together, man shouldn't put asunder. He spoke against divorce and against remarriage, saying that it was committing adultery.

5. **A.** Pope Pius XI says that the mutual molding of a husband and wife, the determined effort to perfect each other, is the chief reason and purpose of matrimony.

   **B.** Answers will vary.

## Lesson 4, Day Two

1. Answers will vary.

2. **Proverbs 12:18** "There is one whose rash words are like sword thrusts, but the tongue of the wise brings healing."

   **Proverbs 15:1** "A soft answer turns away wrath, but a harsh word stirs up anger."

   **Isaiah 50:4** "The lord God has given me the tongue of those who are taught, that I may know how to sustain with a word him that is weary. Morning by morning he wakens, he wakens my ear to hear as those who are taught."

   **Proverbs 29:11** "A fool gives full vent to his anger, but a wise man quietly holds it back."

   **Ephesians 4:15** "Rather, speaking the truth in love, we are to grow up in every way into him who is the head, into Christ."

3. **A.** Answers will vary.

**B.** "Death and life are in the power of the tongue, and those who love it will eat its fruits." (Proverbs 18:21)

4. In Mark 12:31, Jesus tells us to "love your neighbor as yourself."
Answers will vary.

## Lesson 4, Day Three

1. **A.** We can have confidence because there is hope. We will be protected and can rest in safety.
   **B.** Psalm 71:5 tells us that God is our hope. Hope is not wishful thinking or optimism. Hope is a person—"Christ Jesus our hope" (1 Timothy 1:1).
2. **A.** According to 1 Peter 1:3, we are born anew to a living hope.
   **B.** We are born anew to a living hope because of the resurrection of Jesus Christ.
3. Answers will vary.
4. **A.** The wise man builds his house on the rock.
   **B.** She hears Jesus' words and puts them into practice.
   **C.** Answers will vary.

## Lesson 4, Day Four

1. We're told to offer our bodies as a living sacrifice, and doing so is described as a form of worship. Living this way is countercultural, but Saint Paul encourages us in Romans 12:2 to "not be conformed to this world but be transformed by the renewal of [our minds]." If we will do this, we'll be rewarded by growth in understanding of God's will.
2. **A.** We should never be motivated by selfishness or conceit. The virtue we should display is humility, which is seen through considering others better than ourselves.
   **B.** Answers will vary.
   **C.** Jesus is to be our example. Though He was and is equal to God, He never grasped at that equality, and instead, emptied himself and became a servant. He humbled himself to the point of obediently being willing to die on the cross.
3. **Matthew 16:24** "Then Jesus told his disciples, 'If any man would come after me, let him deny himself and take up his cross and follow me.'"
   **Ephesians 5:1–2** "Therefore be imitators of God, as beloved children. And walk in love, as Christ loved us and gave himself up for us, a fragrant offering and sacrifice to God."
4. **A.** "Now I rejoice in my sufferings for your sake, and in my flesh I complete what is lacking in Christ's afflictions for the sake of his body, that is, the Church." (Colossians 1:24)

**B.** The sentences that should be underlined are: "The sufferings of Christ created the good of the world's redemption. This good is in itself inexhaustible and infinite. No man can add anything to it," and "Does this mean that the redemption achieved by Christ is not complete? No."

**C.** Answers will vary.

## Lesson 4, Day Five

1. **Matthew 6:14–15** If we forgive others, God will forgive us. But if we do not forgive others, then it blocks God's forgiveness of us.
   **Matthew 18:21–22** We are not to limit how many times we are willing to forgive.

2. **Romans 12:19** tells us not to seek revenge but instead to "leave it to the wrath of God."

3. **Sirach 28:2–3** Lack of forgiveness not only prevents our sins from being pardoned by God, it also blocks healing from the Lord.
   **Matthew 18:23–34** If we refuse to forgive, we end up imprisoned by bitterness, anger, and loneliness.
   **Ephesians 4:26–27** We give the devil an opportunity to mess with our marriages.

4. Answers will vary.

## Lesson 5, Day One

1. **A.** When God found His children in the wilderness, He encircled them and cared for them. He kept them as the apple of His eye—-a description of delight. God is described as an eagle stirring up its nest, getting the baby birds ready to fly. But as they falter, He comes below them and catches them, carrying them on His wings.

   **B.** We can encircle a child and care for them when they are afraid ("in the wilderness") by physically holding them. Physical touch is critical in these years. Keeping them as the apple of our eye, we can delight in them. Practically speaking, we do this by paying attention to our facial expressions—lighting up and smiling when we look at our children. As they begin to be independent in small ways, we "stir the nest," letting them try, but being nearby to help them if they fail. We catch them and encourage them for trying, instead of doing things for them that they are capable of, or getting angry when they fall short.

2. **A.** God teaches His children to walk, and picks them up in His arms. He is behind the scenes, healing His children, although they don't realize it. God leads His children with compassion. He is described as "one who raises an infant to his cheeks," who bends down to them and feeds them.

    **B.** We teach our children to walk and whatever else is needed for their next stage of development. We help them heal from their hurts, listening to what makes them afraid and causes them pain. We take these things seriously and respond instead of ignoring their cries. We lead with compassion rather than sharp correction and condemnation. We are physically affectionate with our children.

**3.** **A.** God disciplines those He loves, so we shouldn't despise it or grow weary from His correction. Our discipline of our children should be one of the ways we show our delight in them.

    **B.** God disciplines us for our good, so we can become holy. While discipline is painful in the short term, later it helps us to be trained in righteousness.

    **C.** Answers will vary.

**4.** Answers will vary.

## Lesson 5, Day Two

**1.** **A.** God's words are first to be impressed on our own hearts.

    **B.** Answers will vary.

**2.** We are to teach that God is one LORD, and that we are to love Him with all our heart, soul, and mind.

**3.** We are to talk about them when we sit in our homes, when we are walking, when we lie down, and when we rise. We are to bind these words as a sign on our hands, and as a frontlet between our eyes. They are to be written on the doorposts of our homes and gates.

**4.** **A.** God is concerned that during times of prosperity, His children will forget Him. Instead of recognizing that all they have (cities, houses, cisterns, vineyard, olive trees and food) has come from God's generous hands, they will credit themselves.

    **B.** Answers will vary.

## Lesson 5, Day Three

**1.** **A.** Answers will vary.

    **B.** Ephesians 2:10 says that we are God's workmanship, created in Christ Jesus for good works.

Psalm 139:13–16 teaches us that God is our Creator, forming us in our mothers' wombs. It states that we are "wondrously made"—the opposite of a mistake. Verse 16 reminds us that God has written every one of our days in His book—He is in control of our lives.

**2.** **A.** Answers will vary.

B. This verse tells us that the way God measures worth is not based on outward appearance or ability—it's what is on the inside that matters.

3. A. Answers will vary.

B. We might think we need friends' approval to be happy, but the truth is found in Nehemiah 8:10: "Rejoicing in the Lord is your strength." We're told in 1 Corinthians 16:13–14, "Be on your guard, stand firm in the faith, be courageous, be strong. Your every act should be done with love." Doing these things will not usually win you the approval of the crowd, but long term, it will bring you happiness because these are the good and right decisions.

4. A. Answers will vary.

B. In Psalm 37:4 we learn that when we find our delight in God, He gives us the desires of our hearts. In John 10:10 we are told that the enemy is a thief who comes to steal and destroy. By contrast, Jesus comes so that we can have abundant life.

5. Answers will vary.

## Lesson 5, Day Four

1. A. When we pray, we are drawing on the riches of God's glory, and through it, God strengthens us through the Holy Spirit "in the inner man" (Ephesians 3:16). As we pray, we are connecting with Christ who dwells in our hearts through faith. This time in God's presence roots and grounds us in His love, so that we can grasp the breadth, length, height, and depth of the love of Christ. What results? We will be "filled with all the fulness of God" (Ephesians 3:19).

B. Prayer gives us the opportunity to come clean with God—to be honest about how we are and what we might need to confess. God meets us in our "inward being" and teaches us wisdom, there in the "secret heart" (Psalm 51:6).

C. Answers will vary.

2. A. We are told to seek the things that are above—to set our minds on things that are above, not on things that are on earth.

B. Sometimes we *want* something to matter most (something like our kids having an engaged, personal faith) but what we have *actually communicated* is that their grades, or athletic success, or happiness is what we truly value. We communicate this (without words) by what we are willing to sacrifice and what we consider to be nonnegotiable.

C. It's described as exchanging the truth about God for a lie and worshipping and serving the creature rather than the Creator.

**3. A.** "By this power of the Spirit, God's children can bear much fruit. He who has grafted us onto the true vine will make us bear 'the fruit of the Spirit: . . . love, joy, peace, patience, kindness, goodness, faithfulness, gentleness, self-control.' 'We live by the Spirit'; the more we renounce ourselves, the more we 'walk by the Spirit.' Through the Holy Spirit we are restored to paradise, led back to the Kingdom of heaven, and adopted as children, given confidence to call God 'Father' and to share in Christ's grace, called children of light and given a share in eternal glory." (CCC 736)

If we are lacking these winsome qualities that make our faith more attractive, we are to turn to the Holy Spirit. He grafts us onto the true vine (Jesus) and causes us to bear the fruit of the Spirit—love, joy, peace, patience, kindness, goodness, faithfulness, gentleness, and self-control.

**B.** Answers will vary.

**4.** We are to tend the people God has put under our care, not begrudgingly, but willingly. Not for "shameful gain" (our own glory), not by domineering over them, but by being a good example.

## Lesson 5, Day Five

**1.** Friends of a paralyzed man sought to bring him to Jesus for healing. They couldn't get him through the door, so they went up on the roof and let him down through the tiles, into Jesus' presence. Jesus saw the faith of the ones who had carried the man to Him.

**2.** Answers will vary.

**3. A.** This passage uses the figure of the water cycle. It illustrates the point that just as rain and snow come down from heaven and serve their purpose on earth, God's Word comes down and does the same. It does not return to him void—it fulfills His purpose. There's something incredible about God's Word that is very different from ours. God can speak something into being. His words create something out of nothing. God's Word has intrinsic power, and when we pray it back to Him, we are reminding Him of what He has promised. God speaks to accomplish a purpose.

**B.** If we ask for anything according to God's will, He hears us. God's Word reflects His will, so when we pray His own words to Him, we can be sure that He hears and will respond.

**4. Ezekiel 11:19** I pray that you would give my loved one a new heart and a new spirit…that You would remove his heart of stone and give him a heart of flesh.

**Acts 26:18** May You open my loved one's eyes and turn her from darkness to light, from the power of Satan to You, so that she may receive forgiveness of sins and a place among those who are sanctified by faith in You.

**2 Timothy 2:25–26** I pray that you would grant my loved one repentance leading to a knowledge of the truth, and he might come to his senses and escape from the snare of the devil.

**John 6:44** God, I know that no one can come to Jesus unless the Father draws them. May You draw my loved one to You.

**Ephesians 3:18–19** May You overwhelm my loved one with the reality of Your love, so that she can "grasp how wide and long and high and deep is the love of Christ, and to know this love that surpasses knowledge."

## Lesson 6, Day One

1. God gave man dominion over the fish, birds, cattle, and all the earth.
2. **A.** They failed to prevail against the enemy in the garden. The worst of predators, sin, entered their home.
   **B.** Answers will vary.
   **C.** Answers will vary.
3. We're told to catch the little foxes in the vineyard, because if we don't, the vineyard will be spoiled.
   Answers will vary.
4. **A.** Both Adam and Eve blamed someone else. Neither took responsibility for their actions. Adam blamed Eve; Eve blamed the serpent.
   **B.** "I will walk with integrity of heart within my house; I will not set before my eyes anything that is base." (Psalms 101:2–3)
   **C.** Answers will vary.

## Lesson 6, Day Two

1. **Proverbs 15:1** "A soft answer turns away wrath, but a harsh word stirs up anger."
   Answers will vary.
   **Proverbs 19:11** "Good sense makes a man slow to anger, and it is to his glory to overlook an offense."
   Answers will vary.
   **Proverbs 21:9** "It is better to live in a corner of the housetop than in a house shared with a contentious woman."
   Answers will vary.
2. Answers will vary.
3. **John 1:12** Those who receive Jesus and believe in His name are children of God.

**Romans 8:16** The Holy Spirit bears witness within us that we are children of God.

**2 Corinthians 5:17** We are a new creation in Christ. The old has gone, the new has come. There is always a fresh start with Jesus—a do-over button.

**Galatians 3:26** In Christ Jesus, we are sons and daughters of God through faith.

**Galatians 4:7** We are no longer slaves, but sons and daughters of God.

4. Answers will vary.

## Lesson 6, Day Three

1. **A.** **1 Corinthians 14:33** God "is not the God of disorder but of peace."

   **1 Corinthians 14:40** God desires that "all things should be done decently and in order."

   **B.** Answers will vary.

2. **A.** **2 Corinthians 2:14–15** God desires that the fragrance of the knowledge of Christ be spread everywhere we go. We are the aroma of Christ among those who are being saved, and those who are perishing.

   **Ephesians 5:1–2** Christ gave Himself up for us as a fragrant offering. We are to be imitators of Him.

   **B.** Answers will vary.

3. **A.** "Better is a dry morsel with quiet than a house full of feasting with strife." (Proverbs 17:1)

   **B.** Answers will vary.

4. We aren't to let the sun go down on our anger, or we will be giving the devil an opportunity to mess with us.

## Lesson 6, Day Four

1. **A.** A wise woman builds her house, but a foolish woman tears hers down with her own hands.

   **B.** Answers will vary.

2. **A.** Wisdom builds the house, understanding establishes it, and knowledge fills the rooms.

   **B.** "The seven gifts of the Holy Spirit are wisdom, understanding, counsel, fortitude, knowledge, piety and fear of the Lord. They belong in their fullness to Christ, Son of David. They complete and perfect the virtues of those who receive them. They make the faithful docile in readily obeying divine inspirations. Let your good spirit lead me on a level path. For all who are led by the Spirit of God are sons of God . . . If children, then heirs, heirs of God and fellow heirs with Christ." (CCC 1831)

Wisdom, understanding and knowledge are three of the seven gifts of the Holy Spirit.

**Knowledge:** Growing in knowledge has everything to do with what we are choosing to put in our minds. What are we reading? What are we listening to? What are we watching on our screens? Feed your mind with good literature, read Scripture, listen to rich podcasts. Determine to be a lifelong learner. Stop consuming garbage. It's a waste of time and clutters your mind.

**Understanding:** We grow in understanding when we increase of understanding of what God thinks of things. Growth in knowledge can be very dependent on human perspectives. This has its place, but if we fail to give priority to what God says, we will lack understanding. The Bible, spiritual books, and podcasts from good priests and Bible teachers all help us grow in understanding. The sacraments also supernaturally strengthen us to be open and receptive to God's truth.

**Wisdom:** Spiritual Direction is an excellent way to grow in wisdom, as it allows a trained, spiritually mature person to speak into your life in specific, practical ways. Spending time with older mentors who are living out the Christian life authentically is also important. We grow in wisdom when we ask lots of questions and listen. When you see someone you admire and whose life you would like to emulate, ask them questions about their own decisions, priorities, and deepest held values.

3. Answers will vary.
4. Proverbs 31:26 tells us that when we open our mouths, wisdom should be what comes out. Our teaching should be kind, rather than harsh and judgmental.

## Lesson 6, Day Five

1. **A.** Jesus says that when we pray, we are to go into our room and shut the door and pray to your Father who is in secret.
   **B.** Answers will vary.
   **C.** "And in the morning, a great while before day, he rose and went out to a lonely place, and there he prayed." (Mark 1:35)
2. **A.** Where our treasure is, that's where our heart is as well.
   **B.** "We have this treasure in earthen vessels, to show that the transcendent power belongs to God and not to us." (2 Corinthians 4:7)
3. **A.** Answers will vary.
   **B.** Answers will vary.

4. **A.** "Let not your hearts be troubled; believe in God, believe also in me. In my Father's house are many rooms; if it were not so, would I have told you that I go to prepare a place for you? And when I go and prepare a place for you, I will come again and take you to myself, that where I am you may be also." (John 14:1–3)

   **B.** "'Behold, the dwelling of God is with men. He will dwell with them, and they shall be his people, and God himself will be with them; he will wipe away every tear from their eyes, and death shall be no more, neither shall there be mourning nor crying nor pain any more, for the former things have passed away.' And he who sat upon the throne said, 'Behold, I make all things new.'" (Revelation 21:3–5)

## Lesson 7, Day One

1. Answers will vary.
2. **A.** We are to leave our father and mother and cleave to our spouse, becoming one flesh.

   **B.** Answers will vary.
3. **A.** **Colossians 3:20** Children are to obey their parents.
   **Exodus 20:12** We are to honor our father and mother.

   **B.** **Leviticus 19:32** "You shall rise up before the hoary head, and honor the face of an old man, and you shall fear your God: I am the lord."
   **Proverbs 16:31** "A hoary head is crown of glory; it is gained in a righteous life."
   **Proverbs 23:22** "Listen to your father who begot you, and do not despise your mother when she is old."
   **1 Timothy 5:8** "If anyone does not provide for his relatives, and especially for his own family, he has disowned the faith and is worse than an unbeliever."
4. **Psalm 27:10** If or when your father and mother forsake you (which can mean hurting, disappointing, abusing, neglecting, or abandoning), the Lord promises to take care of you.

   **Psalm 68:5–6** God is the Father of the fatherless and the protector of widows. He gives the desolate a home to dwell in. Some translations read "he sets the lonely in families." These verses remind us that God knows we need healthy family interactions. Sometimes we get that from our biological family. Sometimes we need it from an adopted family or a church family. Be assured that God sees what you need and is at work to provide it.

5. "Do nothing from selfishness or conceit, but in humility count others better than yourselves. Let each of you look not only to his own interests but also to the interests of others." (Philippians 2:3–4)

## Lesson 7, Day Two

1. **A. Proverbs 13:20** We should look for wisdom in our friends because those who walk with the wise become wise, and those who spend a lot of time with foolish people start to reflect those qualities. We become like our friends.
   **Proverbs 18:24** We should look for loyalty in a friend.
   **Proverbs 22:24–25** We should pay attention to whether a person is easily angered because we start to reflect that behavior ourselves when we spend a lot of time with an angry friend.
   **1 Corinthians 15:33** We should look for good character in a friend.
   **B.** Answers will vary.
2. **A.** We are to love others deeply, forgiving sin. We are to offer hospitality and use our gifts to serve others.
   **B.** They are helping each other up.
   Answers will vary.
3. **A.** We are to encourage one another and build each another up.
   **B.** Answers will vary.
4. "Faithful are the wounds of a friend." (Proverbs 27:6)

## Lesson 7, Day Three

1. In Genesis 2:15, the Lord put man in the Garden of Eden to work and take care of it. In Genesis 3:3–6, we read about the fall of man, where man sins by eating the forbidden fruit. In Genesis 3:17–18, we read about the curse, the consequence for man's sin. Because of man's sin, work is going to be difficult. The command to work comes before the fall and before the curse.
2. **Ecclesiastes 4:6** This verse describes a person as having two hands full of toil (work), but it isn't sufficient; it's a striving after the wind. You never get there. It's never enough.
   **Proverbs 6:10–11** These verses paint a picture of a person who wants a nap, needs to take yet another break, and fails to do the work that the moment requires.
3. **A.** Solomon says it's better to have a little with fear of the Lord than to have great wealth with turmoil and trouble.
   **B. Psalm 127:2** God gives sleep to those He loves. Much of our rising early, toiling anxiously (key word *anxiously*), and getting to bed late is not within God's will.

**Proverbs 23:4** "Do not toil to acquire wealth; be wise enough to desist." Be wise enough to know when to quit.

**1 Timothy 6:9–10** "Those who desire to be rich fall into temptation, into a snare, into many senseless and hurtful desires that plunge men into ruin and destruction. For the love of money is the root of all evils; it is through this craving that some have wandered away from the faith and pierced their hearts with many pangs."

**Hebrews 13:5** "Keep your life free from love of money, and be content with what you have; for he has said, 'I will never fail you nor forsake you.'"

4.  Saint Paul asks if the reader is seeking man's approval, and notes that if that is what we are after, we are going to have a hard (if not impossible) time serving Christ. Answers will vary.

## Lesson 7, Day Four

1.  "Whatever your task, work heartily, as serving the Lord and not men." (Colossians 3:23)
2.  **A.** This verse is called the Great Commission, and applies to us all. Jesus said, "Go therefore and make disciples of all nations, baptizing them in the name of the Father and of the Son and of the Holy Spirit, teaching them to observe all that I have commanded you; and behold, I am with you always, to the close of the age" (Matthew 28:19–20).
    **B.** Answers will vary.
3.  **A.** Matthew 10:16 says, "Behold, I send you out as sheep in the midst of wolves; so be wise as serpents and innocent as doves."
    **B.** Answers will vary.
    **C.** Answers will vary.
4.  **A.** God's grace is sufficient for us, and His power is made perfect in our weakness.
    **B.** Saint Paul's words in 1 Corinthians 3:5–6 reminds us that it isn't all up to us. Some of us plant a seed, others water, some get the joy of seeing the growth. But in all things and at all times, it is God (not us) who is responsible for the growth. This means that we can do our best, and trust God with the results.

## Lesson 7, Day Five

1.  **A.** We are described as "ambassadors for Christ." God has chosen to make his appeal to mankind through us. The message we've been entrusted with is one of reconciliation to God.
    **B.** Answers will vary.

2.  **A.** The two types of messengers described are a bad messenger and a faithful envoy. A bad messenger plunges men into trouble, but a faithful envoy brings healing.

    **B.** Answers will vary.

3.  **A.** We are to be identified by our love for one another.

    **B.** Answers will vary.

    **C.** Answers will vary.

4.  **A.** Galatians 2:20 says, "I have been crucified with Christ. It is no longer I who live, but Christ who lives in me. And the life I now live in the flesh I live by faith in the Son of God, who loved me and gave himself for me." In a mysterious way, through grace, Christ lives within us and does in and through us what we cannot do on our own.

    **B.** Acts 1:8 says, "You will receive power when the Holy Spirit comes upon you, and you will be my witnesses in Jerusalem, throughout Judea and Samaria, and to the ends of the earth." According to CCC 733 "'God is love' and love is his first gift, containing all others. 'God's love has been poured into our hearts through the Holy Spirit who has been given to us.'"

# Prayer Pages

## walking with purpose

### *Ordering Your Priorities Prayer*

Dear Lord,

Help me to discover what matters most in life, and how to prioritize
those things.  May I "stand by the roads, and look, and ask for
the ancient paths, where the good way is; and walk in it"
(Jeremiah 6:16).

May I put You first. May I "be like a wise man who built
his house upon the rock;  and the rain fell, and the floods
came, and the winds blew and beat upon that house,  but it
did not fall, because it had been founded on the rock"
(Matthew 7:24–25).

"Lead me to the rock that is higher than I; for you are
my refuge, a strong tower against the enemy"
(Psalm 61:2–3).

May I value people over projects, because I "look not to the things
that are seen but to the things that are unseen;  for the things that
are seen are transient, but the things that are unseen are eternal"
(2 Corinthians 4:18).

I acknowledge my limitations and trust You with all that's
undone,  knowing that You "who began a good work in [me]
will bring it to completion at the day of Jesus Christ"
(Philippians 1:6).

You said, "I came that they may have life, and have it abundantly"
(John 10:10). May I experience all the abundance You've promised.
Amen.

# Prayer Requests

Date:

Date:

# Prayer Requests

Date:

Date:

# *Prayer Requests*

Date:

***

Date:

# Prayer Requests

Date:

Date:

*"For to the one who has, more will be given"*
*Matthew 13:12*

# The Journey Doesn't End Here

## ~ Christ's Love Is Endless ~

Walking with Purpose is more than a Bible study, it's a supportive community of women seeking lasting transformation of the heart. And you are invited.

Walking with Purpose believes that change happens in the hearts of women – and, by extension, in their families and beyond – through Bible study and community. We welcome all women, irrespective of faith background, age, or marital status.

Connect with us online for regular inspiration and to join the conversation. There you'll find insightful blog posts, videos, and free scripture printables.

For a daily dose of spiritual nourishment, join our community on Facebook, Twitter, Pinterest and Instagram.

And if you're so moved to start a Walking with Purpose study group at home or in your parish, take a look at our website for more information.

**walkingwithpurpose.com**

walking with purpose
~ SO MUCH MORE THAN A BIBLE STUDY ~

# The guided tour of God's love begins here.

*Opening Your Heart: The Starting Point* begins a woman's exploration of her Catholic faith and enhances her relationship with Jesus Christ. This Bible study is designed to inspire thoughtful consideration of the fundamental questions of living a life in the Lord. More than anything, it's a weekly practice of opening your heart to the only One who can heal and transform lives.

**Explore these topics and more:**

- What is the role of the Holy Spirit in my life?
- What does the Eucharist have to do with my friendship with Christ?
- What are the limits of Christ's forgiveness?
- Why and how should I pray?
- What is the purpose of suffering?
- What challenges will I face in my efforts to follow Jesus more closely?
- How can fear be overcome?

A companion video series complements this journey with practical insights and spiritual support.

*Opening Your Heart* is a foundational 22-lesson Bible study that serves any woman who seeks to grow closer to God. It's an ideal starting point for women who are new to Walking with Purpose and those with prior practice in Bible study, too.

To share Walking with Purpose with the women in your parish, contact us at walkingwithpurpose.com/contact-us.

**walkingwithpurpose.com**

walking with purpose

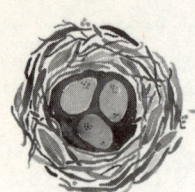

# Transformative Catholic Bible Studies

Walking with Purpose Bible studies are created to help women deepen their personal relationship with Christ. Each study includes many lessons that explore core themes and challenges of modern life through the ancient wisdom of the Bible and the Catholic Church.

### Opening Your Heart

A thoughtful consideration of the fundamental questions of faith – from why and how to pray to the role of the Holy Spirit in our lives and the purpose of suffering.

### Living In the Father's Love

Gain a deeper understanding of how God's unconditional love transforms your relationship with others, with yourself, and most dearly, with Him.

### Keeping In Balance

Discover how the wisdom of the Old and New Testaments can help you live a blessed lifestyle of calm, health, and holiness.

### Touching the Divine

These thoughtful lessons draw you closer to Jesus and deepen your faith, trust, and understanding of what it means to be God's beloved daughter.

### Discovering Our Dignity

Modern-day insight directly from women of the Bible presented as a tender, honest, and loving conversation—woman to woman.

### Beholding His Glory

Old Testament Scripture leads us directly to our Redeemer, Jesus Christ. Page after page, God's awe-inspiring majesty is a treasure to behold.

### Beholding Your King

This study of King David and several Old Testament prophets offers a fresh perspective of how all Scripture points to the glorious coming of Christ.

### Grounded In Hope

Anchor yourself in the truth found in the New Testament book of Hebrews, and gain practical insight to help you run your race with perseverance.

### Fearless and Free

With an emphasis on healing and wholeness, this study provides a firm foundation to stand on, no matter what life throws our way.

### Reclaiming Friendship

Let God reshape how you see and experience intentional relationships, deal with your past friendship wounds, and become a woman who is capable of the lifelong bond of true friendship.

**Choose your next Bible study at
shop.walkingwithpurpose.com**

walking with purpose
SO MUCH MORE THAN A BIBLE STUDY

# Share your faith with the next generation

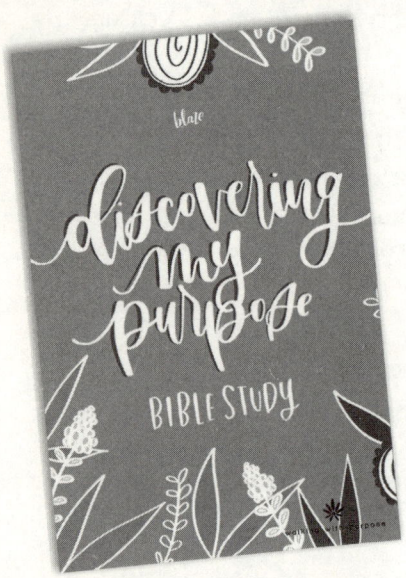

*Discovering My Purpose* is a six-session Bible study designed for girls in their tween/teen years. This Bible study opens girls' eyes to their unique purpose, gifts, and God's love. It includes the BLAZE Spiritual Gifts Inventory, a fabulous tool to help girls discern where God is calling them to be world-changers.

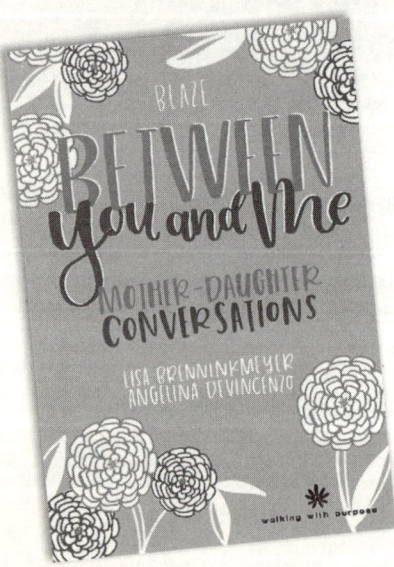

*Between You and Me* is a 40-day conversation guide for mothers and daughters to read together. Each day compares a lie of our secular culture with the truth found in Scripture. The daily reflection, discussion questions, and prayer prompts will springboard the mother/daughter relationship to a new level of honesty and intimacy.

**BLAZE Masterpiece**　　　　　**BLAZE Belong**

- 20-lesson programs designed to help you lead any size group of middle school girls to a closer relationship with Christ.

- Both programs include BLAZE Kits, which are full of fun materials and take-home gifts that correspond with each lesson.

- BLAZE gives you the tools to speak to girls about their true identity as beloved daughters of God!

# Learn more at walkingwithpurpose.com/blaze

walking with purpose

◦～ SO MUCH MORE THAN A BIBLE STUDY ～◦

# Walking with Purpose Devotionals

Daily affirmations of God's love

### Rest: 31 Days of Peace

- A beautiful, hardcover, pocket-sized devotional to take wherever you go.

- 31 Scripture-based meditations that you can read (and re-read) daily.

- Become saturated with the truth that you are seen, known, and loved by a God who gave everything for you!

### Be Still: A Daily Devotional to Quiet Your Heart

- Grow closer to the Lord each day of the year with our 365-day devotional.

- This beautifully designed hardcover devotional collection will renew your mind and help you look at things from God's perspective.

- Apply what you read in *Be Still*, and you'll make significant progress in your spiritual life!

**shop.walkingwithpurpose.com**

**walking with purpose**

SO MUCH MORE THAN A BIBLE STUDY

# *Journal Your Prayers & Grow Closer to God*

The Walking with Purpose *Praying from the Heart: Guided Journal* is a beautiful, comprehensive prayer journal that provides a private space to share your thoughts and feelings with the Lord.

Journaling your prayers lets you express a greater depth of intimacy toward God, and it will help you cultivate the practice of gratitude. Journaling will motivate you to pray regularly, too!

*Praying from the Heart* lays flat for easy writing, and is fashioned after the way that author Lisa Brenninkmeyer journals her own prayers. You'll love the heavyweight paper, luxurious leatherette cover, and many other special details.

**shop.walkingwithpurpose.com**

walking with purpose
SO MUCH MORE THAN A BIBLE STUDY

## ✸ DEEPEN YOUR FAITH ✸ OPEN YOUR ARMS ✸ ✸ BROADEN YOUR CIRCLE ✸

When your heart opens, and your love for Christ deepens, you may be moved to bring Walking With Purpose to your friends or parish. It's rewarding experience for many women who, in doing so, learn to rely on God's grace while serving Him.

**If leading a group seems like a leap of faith, consider that you already have all the skills you need to share the Lord's Word:**

- Personal commitment to Christ
- Desire to share the love of Christ
- Belief in the power of authentic, transparent community

**The Walking With Purpose community supports you with:**

- Training
- Mentoring
- Bible study materials
- Promotional materials

Few things stretch and grow our faith like stepping out of our comfort zone and asking God to work through us. Say YES, soon you'll see the mysterious and unpredictable ways He works through imperfect women devoted to Him.

Remember that if you humbly offer Him what you can, He promises to do the rest.

*"See to it that no one misses the grace of God"* Hebrews 12:15

### Learn more about bringing Walking with Purpose to your parish. Visit us at walkingwithpurpose.com

walking with purpose

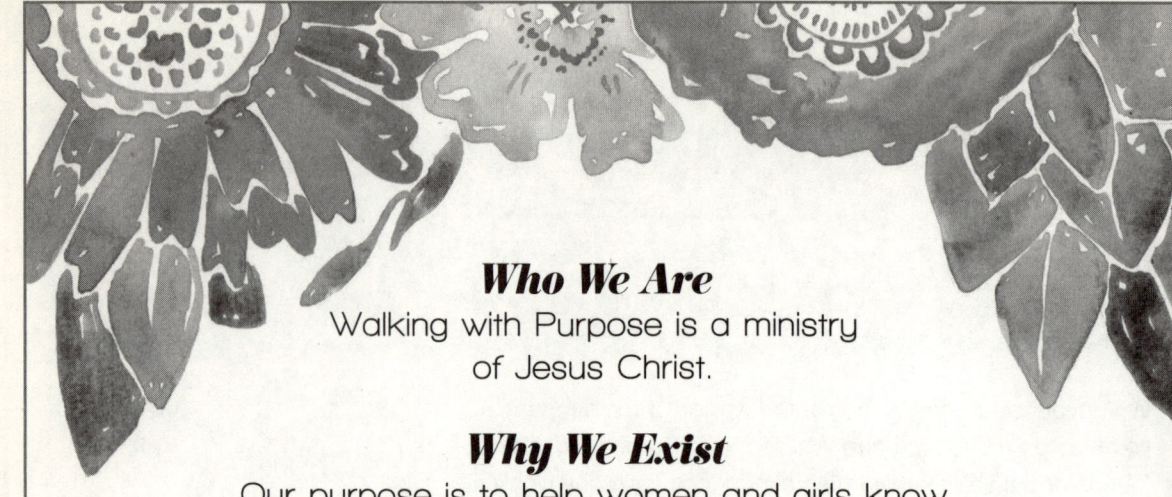

### Who We Are

Walking with Purpose is a ministry
of Jesus Christ.

### Why We Exist

Our purpose is to help women and girls know
Jesus Christ personally by making Scripture and the
teachings of the Catholic Church relevant and applicable.

### Our Mission

Our mission is to help every Catholic woman and girl in
America encounter Jesus Christ through our Bible studies.

### Our Vision

Our vision for the future is that, as more Catholic
women deepen their relationships with Jesus Christ,
eternity-changing transformation will take place in their
hearts – and, by extension – in their families, in their
communities, and ultimately, in our nation.

walking with purpose
SO MUCH MORE THAN A BIBLE STUDY

You can support our mission through a tax-deductible gift.
Learn more at walkingwithpurpose.com/donate